T5-AMY-943

PRAISE FOR *BRAVERY:*
THE LIVING BUDDHA WITHIN YOU

"In this book, Frank Berliner has given us one of the most comprehensive and clear-eyed expositions of the teachings of the Buddha by a Western Buddhist practitioner and teacher. Berliner, a long time student of the renowned Tibetan meditation master, Chögyam Trungpa Rinpoche, has drunk deep from the well of not only his teacher's encyclopedic presentation of the Buddhadharma but also that of Western philosophy, psychology, and literature. This is both an excellent primer and in-depth study of the core elements of Buddhist psychology and philosophy explained with crystalline clarity for the Western student within the context of Western thought, classic and modern. This is a must-read book for serious Buddhist practitioners. It also deserves a central place in any Buddhist studies or Buddhist psychology university curriculum."

FLEET MAULL
senior teacher in both the Shambhala Buddhist lineage and the Zen Peacemaker Order,
founder of Prison Mindfulness Institute, and author of *Dharma in Hell,
the Prison Writings of Fleet Maull* and *Radical Responsibility*

"Mr. Berliner has given us a personal, compelling, and very accessible account of the practice of meditation and the authentic spiritual journey it unlocks. Beautifully written, with warmth, humor, and clarity, this is a book that will be widely read and treasured by many."

REGINALD A. RAY, PhD
spiritual director of the Dharma Ocean Foundation and author of
Touching Enlightenment and *Mahamudra for the Modern World*

"Frank Berliner has distilled a lifetime of learning into an accessible and practical book. Pithy and profound, there is plenty here to benefit anyone interested in the deeper aspects of meditation. There is a light within you—this book can turn it on."

ANDREW HOLECEK
author of *Meditation in the iGeneration: How to Meditate in a World of Speed and Stress*

BRAVERY

For Jim,
and the joy of the
living Buddha within you.

Frank
16 October 2016

Also by Frank W. Berliner

FALLING IN LOVE WITH A BUDDHA

Frank Berliner came of age in the turbulent and exciting era of the 1960s in America, and met the authentic spiritual master Chögyam Trungpa Rinpoche just as the Western cultural door opened to receive the ancient wisdom of Tibetan Buddhism. In *Falling in Love with a Buddha,* Frank recalls the world of Rinpoche's life and teachings. In vivid and often humorous first-person accounts of the founding and evolution of the Shambhala tradition, he evokes the powerful and enigmatic presence of this unique teacher.

At the same time, Frank tells the moving personal story of a father and son. Their relationship is marked by great tenderness, by conflict, and by strokes of mutual insight as Frank's father encounters the inscrutable force field of Chögyam Trungpa. As the cycles of life and death inevitably ripen, the passing of each of these men marks Frank indelibly with their abiding presence in his own life.

This book brings to life again a potent moment in cultural history, and helps us more fully appreciate this revolutionary teacher and his profound impact on the lives of his students. Finally, it deepens our understanding of a genuine, heartfelt spiritual path by revealing the intimate ways our personal awakening can touch those closest to us.

BRAVERY

Living THE Buddha
Within You

Frank W. Berliner

All My Relations
Boulder, Colorado

*This book is dedicated to the eternal youth
of the living Buddha within each of us.*

All My Relations, LLC
Boulder, Colorado

©2014 Frank W. Berliner
Published by All My Relations, LLC

All rights reserved. No part of this book may be reproduced or transmitted
in any form or by any means, electronic or mechanical, including photocopying,
recording, or by any information storage and retrieval system, without written
permission from the author.

First Edition
Printed in the United States of America

Cover and book design by Beth Skelley

ISBN 978-0-9851790-2-1
Ebook ISBN 978-0-9851790-3-8

10 9 8 7 6 5 4 3 2 1

CONTENTS

INTRODUCTION

I t is only very recently that the mindfulness meditation of the Buddha has begun to enter the mainstream of American life. It remains to be seen whether this will be a long-term phenomenon or a passing fad in our consumer culture. Certainly it is a very positive development. Even this small gesture toward slowing down, paying closer attention to the inner world of thoughts and emotions, and reducing tension can benefit each of us. But this is only an initial step into the vast landscape of meditative training. The Buddhist tradition out of which the new, American adaptations have come is primordial, challenging, and profound.

It is primordial because human beings have been practicing it for a very long time. Of course the mere fact of this does not automatically confer value. More significant is that this practice has been handed down orally from teacher to student throughout that time in many different cultures around the world. While it is ancient, it is not archaic and is always fresh and up-to-date. It is a vibrant, living tradition, based not on creeds or dogma, but on direct personal experience.

It is challenging because the wholehearted willingness to face your heart and mind as a lifelong discipline will inevitably bring you to places within yourself that require bravery to confront, to remain present with, and to befriend. Making friends fully with all the hidden recesses of your heart and mind is certainly the most arduous task—yet at the same time the most precious gift—that you can possibly experience in life. My own teacher referred to it as "the path of the warrior."[1] By this, he meant the warrior who makes peace through bravery and gentleness, not the warrior who makes war out of cowardice.

It is profound because it has the potential to give you access to an unimaginably transformative level of awareness, insight, love, and connection with others in your life. In those individuals who have fully embodied the commitment to this practice, the fruits of all this are unmistakable and inspiring. These rare individuals show us what life as a fully human being looks like, feels like, and is. They also remind us that we can do the same, if we have the faith and the exertion to try.

This book is the result of the impact of such a human being on my own life. My spiritual teacher, Chögyam Trungpa Rinpoche, was a meditation master in the Tibetan Buddhist tradition whose life and work have done much to plant the complete teachings and practices of Buddhism in the cultural soil of this country. In the pages that follow, I have attempted to communicate some of the essence of what he taught me, to mix it with my personal experience, and perhaps with yours as well.

As it is traditionally and truly said, all benefit that may come from this book is due solely to my teacher, and all faults are my own. May there be benefit!

Frank W. Berliner
April 2014

PART ONE

WHAT WE WANT
AND WHAT WE ARE

The Living Buddha within You

It takes courage to lead an authentic life in this world. There are so many sidetracks that steal away our resolve and our commitment to do so. Driven to material gain and distracted from what matters, we find ourselves in a world where the wisdom that might guide us toward this genuineness has been ignored and almost lost. What the poet William Wordsworth wrote two hundred years ago is more timely now than ever:

> The world is too much with us; late and soon,
> Getting and spending, we lay waste our powers . . . [2]

But in our heart of hearts, many of us never give up our longing for wisdom.

Twenty-five hundred years ago, a young aristocrat from a powerful family in northern India resolved to follow this longing's call. He abandoned the life that had been prepared for him, perceiving it clearly as a gilded cage. He set out to find his own truth. He searched resolutely for his own answer to the perennial existential question that human beings will never stop asking: *In the brief time that I have on this earth, what is most important, and how shall I live in a way that honors it?*

In the time that has passed since he lived, what he discovered has influenced and guided countless others. But only in the past fifty years has the map for this discovery been available to us in the West.

That young aristocrat was the Buddha. He wasn't born with that name. He received it from others who recognized immediately that the genuineness he had discovered was radiating out from his life in every word and every gesture. Quite simply, he was completely awake—which is what the word *buddha* means.

DEMOCRACY OF INHERENT WAKEFULNESS

The wonderful news is that each of us has the potential to make the same discovery that the Buddha did. The living Buddha within you is the ultimate expression of democracy. Thomas Jefferson wrote about democracy in a way that has inspired millions of people all over the world. He wrote that we are all created equal and endowed by our Creator with the inalienable rights of life, liberty, and the pursuit of happiness.

The Buddha would have described the matter slightly differently.

Instead of a Declaration of Independence, he might have called his discovery a Proclamation of Wakefulness. He would have reminded us that this wakefulness is not bestowed by someone else. Instead, it is fundamental to who we are as human beings. Rather than pointing to our inalienable rights, he would have described our deepest inherent qualities, such as bravery, kindness, and wisdom.

But like the oil inside a sesame seed, this wakefulness inside us must be extracted if we are to enjoy it fully.

The living Buddha within you is hidden beneath layers of hope and fear, doubt and distraction, and especially the habit of not paying enough attention to what is happening within you and around you, right now. You must gently but persistently peel away these layers so that you experience the rich nourishment at your core. No one else can do this for you.

Seeking wisdom is like being a diner who is planning a visit to a fine restaurant for the first time. You can read the menu and imagine all the delicious meals you might order, but until you have actually tasted the food, chewed it, and eaten it, you will still be hungry.

The Journey without Goal

My spiritual master liked to say that our path to enlightenment is a journey without goal. Therefore, you are embarking on an endless journey. It is endless because every goal you may feel you have accomplished simply opens the gateway to yet a further territory that you have not explored. So there is never a final destination.

He also said that your teacher is never going to congratulate you when you become enlightened. Because there is no finish line, there are no final congratulations.

Throughout our lives, the world sets goals and standards for us that we strive to achieve, and judges us as successes or failures based on whether or not we accomplish them.

But it is common even for successful people—once they have reached their goal—to feel that it wasn't quite what they wanted. There is an underlying sense of dissatisfaction, a gnawing feeling that there must be more to life than their accomplishments. So the journey continues, new goals are set, which lays the ground for further success or failure, and further dissatisfaction down the road. It is simply another endless journey.

At heart, then, is the spiritual path so different from a worldly path if it turns out there is no final goal for either?

To walk on a genuine path of awakening, you need to accept this as being true right from the beginning. You embark on the journey knowing that it has no real end and that no goal you attain will give you permanent satisfaction. Yet at the same time you discover, more and more, that there are tremendous feelings of inspiration and humor and joy in the journey without goal that can only happen when you stop fixating tightly on an end result. And the more you experience this, the more you realize that you are not living for the destination, but for the journey itself.

Here is one way you might take the teachings and make them into a goal. My teacher, Chögyam Trungpa Rinpoche, described the path in this way: "Spirituality is cutting through hope and fear, as well as being the sudden discovery of intelligence that goes along with this process."[3]

He also said that to be a master spiritual warrior is to live beyond hope and fear altogether. With these teachings, he seems to be asking us to see the direct connection between our hope and fear, and the importance we assign to all the goals we set for ourselves in life. He also wants us to perceive how much we feel is at stake.

When Chögyam Trungpa taught, an underlying message was always present: "If you really want to understand spirituality, *lighten up a little!*" Reading such a statement, you might fixate on that goal and say to yourself: *I will move completely beyond hope and fear. I will lighten up!*

And, of course, this would miss the point.

Rather than trying to proclaim the total eradication of hope and fear as a glorious finale for all your spiritual efforts, it is more useful to look at the pervasive presence of hope and fear in your life right now and see what this might have to teach you.

JOURNEYING AS A HUMAN BEING

When you look directly and honestly at your life in this way, you inevitably witness your discomfort with your experience. There is an inherent tension in being human. This is not to say that we are walking around totally uptight all the time, but that at a very deep level, there is an inner conflict embedded in the very fact that we are alive, and we cannot escape it.

The tension is the conflict between our endless longing for happiness and the finite condition that we find ourselves in as mortal humans. Despite an unquenchable thirst for the complete fulfillment of your desires, you must also continuously face the painful facts of life such as loss, aging, illness, and death—which remind you again and again of the limitations of being human. The Greek philosopher Heraclitus observed that our life is nothing but an endless desire to live and an endless dissatisfaction with living.

On one hand, the tension is inescapable. On the other, the tension is noble. There is real nobility in it; there is nobility in the fact that this is what you are faced with if you are honest about life at its deepest level. Indeed, the Buddha himself referred to this tension as the First Noble Truth of life. He called it "the truth of suffering."

From a conventional point of view, just to say this—to acknowledge the truth of it—is threatening and even a bit shocking. It is threatening because we live in a world where this kind of honest conversation is rarely engaged. In fact, there is a sort of ongoing conspiracy of silence that prevents us from talking about this. Instead, we keep compulsively busy in our determination to ignore the whole subject. As the poet Pablo Neruda wrote:

> If we were not so singleminded
> about keeping our lives moving,
> and for once could do nothing,
> perhaps a huge silence

might interrupt this sadness
of never understanding ourselves
and of threatening ourselves with death.[4]

It is very, very difficult for any of us to look deeply at the things that create our underlying tension without turning away.

Because you are human, you long for happiness and hope arises. With awareness of your limitations—and especially your awareness of the certainty of your death—fear arises. And as the poet Philip Larkin memorably wrote,

This is a special way of being afraid
No trick dispels . . . [5]

Because this tension is always there, you experience hope and fear, all the time. This alternation between the two is a pendulum that swings back and forth continuously in your life. There is no one in this world who does not experience this. For this reason, it's not hope itself that is the problem. It's not the fear itself that is the problem. Rather, the real source of your pain is the way you *struggle* with them.

Consider your experience. You try to get rid of the fear and enshrine the hope; you try to banish the uncertainty and fortify the comfort and security. But your struggle to hold on to one and get rid of the other just makes the problem worse.

This is the shifting ground you stand on when you tell yourself you want to be "enlightened" or "liberated"—or any such lofty aspiration. The shiftiness is not the result of some deficiency in you. It is built into your existential predicament. You must begin just where you are—where all of us are—as a creature trapped in the net of hope and fear, struggling to break free.

Jean-Paul Sartre lamented, "Man is a useless passion."[6] Having spent his life looking deeply at the tension I've been describing, this was Sartre's conclusion. His compatriot Albert Camus added, "Life is absurd . . . The only serious philosophical question is suicide."[7] Yet neither of them took their own insights so literally that they killed themselves or even threw up their hands in despair. Instead, each lived with passionate engagement in political resistance or social revolution and his generation's cultural and intellectual life.

The Buddha looked at the same tension, but came to a different conclusion. He recommended that—in order to be a genuine human being, as shifty and full of suffering as we are—we take a different course of action. He recommended that we journey without a goal.

PLEASING ILLUSIONS
THAT PUT US TO SLEEP

The power of materialism, particularly in the West but increasingly all over the world, is pervasive. When my teacher first began sharing authentic wisdom in America, he started by emphasizing the reality of this power and how important it is for all of us on a genuine spiritual path to have a realistic understanding of the ways it challenges us.

Materialism has become the main strategy for attempting to resolve our tension between our longing and our limitation, our hope and our fear. Through its emphasis on comfort, security, and efficiency—and its ability to provide these for people all over the world—materialism induces the illusion that this tension is no longer an issue because our modern world empowers us to provide ourselves with a pleasant lifestyle.

But this is not the case. Just as hope and fear, each in itself, are not the problem, we do not need to make the moral judgment that materialism is an inherently bad thing. While it is increasingly true that technological and material "progress" bring with them a host of new social and environmental problems, these are not the concerns I wish to address in this book. Materialism is not a bad thing so much as a limited thing; it is the wrong tool for the job, like using a hammer to saw a piece of wood. Materialism does not offer a real solution to our underlying human tension.

Let's look more closely at how and why this is the case. My teacher shared with us a traditional Tibetan teaching that describes three lords of materialism. The word *lords* here connotes the feudal sense—masters over their domains, with us as their serfs. So lordship here indicates a relationship based on domination and oppression.

These lords rule on three levels: physical, psychological, and spiritual. They all absorb us in an ongoing project of bringing what, in their view, is an unpredictable and often dangerous world under human control.[8]

Human beings have a natural tendency to evolve from one level of materialism into the next. Having mastered one level, we are drawn inevitably to focus on a more sophisticated or subtle level, and we keep going forward in that way with our fundamental evolutionary instinct.

PHYSICAL MATERIALISM

To begin, we engage physical materialism—which is initially the pursuit of material necessities and ultimately becomes the preoccupation with wealth, comfort, and ease.

The first level of materialism, which for the vast majority of humanity is simply *survival,* begins as the essential and necessary preoccupations that allow human life to continue. But once survival is at least temporarily assured, materialism proliferates further in a way that no longer has anything to do with survival. We begin trying to secure our *imagined future.* This shift from present concern to future concern is highly significant: it is when the physical level of materialism becomes a "lord" that rules us.

Under this lord, we feel we need to have more than the necessities, and the need to have more is what brings hope and fear into our life on a more abstract level. Now we are enticed by the mirage, or haunted by the specter, of future possibilities.

But even when we have fulfilled the physical level of materialism to its utmost, we find that this accomplishment has not solved our underlying problem. What persists is a gnawing sense of dissatisfaction and boredom. We feel there must be more to life. There must be something more meaningful than merely having lots of toys—even more toys than anyone else.

In fact, having exhausted wealth's ability to satisfy, we may find ourselves using the power and influence our wealth provides to influence others, but on a different level of materialism—the psychological level.

PSYCHOLOGICAL MATERIALISM

Whether wealthy or not, we may try to bring our world under control with our ideas. We attempt this through the philosophical or political or religious systems of belief with which we feel we can identify and to which we can belong. Theistic systems based on belief in a savior are forms of psychological materialism because we project the ultimate source of safety "out there" onto an All-Powerful Being that is somehow going to save us, or punish us, in the future. This serves the same function as physical materialism, giving the illusion of securing and protecting ourselves with *externals.*

But we encounter the same result. We give away our power to these externals.

These projections then enslave us. As we know from even a quick glance at human history, passion for our own beliefs is extremely dangerous to ourselves and to others. We are willing to kill others over them, and do. In fact, the harm we do to ourselves and to others as a result of our beliefs seems equally as bad as, if not worse than, the harm we do in the competition for physical resources. We are sure we have found *the answer*—whether it is religious or secular—and we want everyone else to have that answer, too. Then to our surprise, we discover that they already have their own answers and are not interested in being converted to ours. The road to hell is paved with our good intentions. This is why the second lord of materialism is even more dangerous to us than the first.

Of course, psychological materialism is not limited to theistic belief systems alone. All intellectual systems, schools, and all political parties and factions have the potential to be used in this way. Since most educated people tend to adopt many philosophical, psychological, and political ideas, and many even depend on promoting these ideas for their livelihood in a materialistic society, it is obviously impractical to approach the problem from the point of view of trying to abolish such things. They are part of our human inheritance, whether we resonate with the worldview of Freud or Jung, Ayn Rand or Karl Marx, Evangelical Christianity or Tibetan Buddhism. The passion, diversity, and liveliness of our intellectual life will always be with us in any "free" society.

The issue here is not that all intellectual systems or traditions are inherently false or flawed, and we should therefore reject them out of hand. The issue is that the truth they point to, by its very nature, is inevitably partial, biased, and incomplete. As a result, our tendency to create our identity around any ideology—no matter how noble or persuasive—narrows our vision and often blocks our capacity to understand and empathize with others' points of view. Our impulse to define ourselves and seek security, approval, power, or admiration for our ideas and opinions—even in the event that it doesn't lead us to actively harm others who see the world differently—ultimately limits our capacity to grow spiritually because it traps us in an adversarial, dualistic model of reality.

The Buddha didn't wake up by taking sides.

DANCING WITH HOPE AND FEAR

Spiritual materialism is the last and most subtle form. Spiritual materialism is your effort to use spiritual *practice*—as opposed to religious, political, or philosophical belief—as a way to create a sense of ultimate security, certainty, and permanence.

The life of the Buddha and the inner journey he made in order to become "buddha"—completely awakened—is a vivid example of the power of spiritual materialism and the courage required to go beyond it.

The Indian society into which he was born had a highly developed spiritual culture based on several thousand years of tradition and practice. In his search for inner knowledge, he was faced constantly with this question: Should I become part of this tradition, or is the truth that I'm looking for somewhere else? Along the way, he encountered three approaches.

TRYING TO BECOME HIGHER

The first materialistic approach to meditation that the Buddha encountered was *trying to become higher*. In this approach, you imagine that you are uniting yourself with a divine principle, a higher being that is going to elevate you from ordinariness into sacredness. Ultimately, you are trying to unite yourself with an ideal that you created to begin with and then projected externally. Having created this sacred projection, you then tell yourself that it is really separate from you, and you strive to unite yourself with it.

Beyond the self-deception involved in creating something that you then regard as an independent reality, you are also practicing with the assumption that you are not already complete as you are and that there's something higher that is going to rescue you from your debased condition. So the whole psychological posture of this kind of practice reinforces your hope that you could become enlightened and your fear that you won't.

CENTRALIZING INWARDS

The second approach the Buddha encountered was *centralizing inwards*. This involves using an object of meditation—such as a flame, sounds, a visualized image, or the breath—to bring the mind to a state of complete focus and absorption, and then dwelling there as long as possible.

By doing this, the fickle and unpredictable energy of both the outer world and the inner world is excluded from the realm of meditation. Because you can sustain a state of absorption for very long periods of time, once again, there is a subtle hope that you can sustain it indefinitely and a fear that you will not be able to do so.

What the Buddha discovered in these two forms of spiritual materialism is that, like everything else in the universe, these states are subject to impermanence and sooner or later they will fall apart. Whether your effort is to unite yourself with something higher or to absorb yourself by centralizing inwards, the power of the fickleness of impermanence is always present. It will undermine your attempts to achieve a permanent inner state of any kind.

COMPLETELY IDENTIFYING WITH NOWNESS

The meditation that the Buddha finally explored in his courageous journey to free himself from any trace of spiritual materialism is *completely identifying with nowness.* This approach involves resting continuously in the experience of the present moment, whatever it may bring. In this practice there is no aim to become higher and no attempt to create a special meditative cocoon through absorption. This is not to say that these methods or techniques cannot be used, but they are used with a very different attitude. That is, they are used only in the service of identifying the mind with the present moment.

As the practice of meditation has gained more of a foothold in the West, it has become almost a cliché for people to talk about the importance of "being in the present moment," as if it is some magical and quick path to understanding the true meaning of life and making it as painless as possible. But Westerners often don't have much genuine understanding of what their words actually mean.

According to the Buddha, "being in the present moment" means that whatever life is offering in the moment—whether hope or fear, pleasure or pain, joy or sadness, success or failure, or anything in between—*that* is your object of practice. Your present moment may not always be a glass of cabernet; it may be a dose of chemotherapy.

CUT OFF FROM THE LIVING WORLD

The underlying promise of materialism is that it can fulfill all your longing and banish all your anxiety. But it cannot ultimately keep that promise. By putting your faith in the "lords" of materialism, you agree to be enslaved by them in a cycle of promise and disappointment that is never ending. As a slave, what is it that you agree to surrender? You barter away your fundamental vitality and innate confidence in exchange for the illusion of security they offer.

To understand why this is so, consider the underlying motivation for all forms of materialism, which is to control your world—outer or inner—so that you can be permanently safe. To assure yourself of this safety, you must separate yourself from the thing that you think you need to control. What we call the *material* world is really just a projection based on this need to separate the world from ourselves in order to manage it at all times.

But the world is a living world. You are embedded in it at all times, and you can never really separate yourself from it. Here it is more accurate to say that you live in an *elemental* world, rather than a material world. This elemental world is composed of earth, water, fire, wind, and space. These elements exist all around you and within you as well. They are full of vitality, constantly shifting and changing. The elemental world, from which you can never separate yourself because you are always part of it, is the real source of your strength.

By pledging your allegiance to materialism, you forfeit your access to that living relationship with the world. The whole path of genuine spirituality is about dropping materialism's imaginary boundary between you and the elemental world and beginning to relate to that world directly.

TRUE MEDICINE FOR SUFFERING

The strategies of materialism ultimately weaken you through distraction. In its obsessive pursuit of the control and manipulation of your immediate experience, materialism cannot offer you the medicine for your suffering. The Dalai Lama has said that the Buddha should be understood as a doctor—rather than as a philosopher or a priest or a savior—and the Dharma that he taught as medicine.

When you go to a doctor, he examines you, and based on what your illness is, he prescribes medicine that you then take. You don't worship the doctor. Worshiping the doctor is not going to do you any good at all. Taking the medicine is what's going to do you good.

Buddhism is a nontheistic path. The doctor doesn't need or want your worship. Indeed, if he or she does, then he is not a genuine doctor. Ultimately, you are alone with the challenge of your personal struggle with hope and fear. Only when you understand the hopelessness of trying to manipulate this challenge, can you truly and honestly embark on the spiritual path.

JOURNEYING THROUGH MATERIALISM WITHOUT GOAL

Be forewarned: your earnest project of trying to eliminate all traces of materialism from your life—thinking that *this* will get you where you want to go—is going to be hopeless as well. That is just another form of manipulating your experience. Rather than rejecting materialism—pretending it's not happening or convincing yourself you are something other than you are or better than that—you accept all this as part of your working basis. This is especially important to acknowledge so that you have a sense of humor about your life and your path and how you too are deeply embedded in the delusions of the materialistic world, along with everyone else.

In other words, you accept your hope and fear as the raw materials of your spiritual path because you have the honesty to admit that your materialistic strategies have not resolved your struggle with them. Then by committing yourself to a practice that's based on being completely identified with nowness, your struggle with hope and fear can become a dance.

As the poet T. S. Eliot put it: "At the still point of the turning world, there the dance is."[9] Meditation is about finding that connection with stillness and with nowness beyond mere projections of the mind. Meditation is not merely a projection of hope or fear, of the past or the future. To fully identify with nowness is to experience life as Eliot describes. You begin to learn how to remain still in the midst of the endless movement of your mind and the world around you.

THE INTELLIGENCE WITHIN YOU

When you open yourself up to nowness fully and allow the whole dance of hope and fear in your life to be there without immediately pushing it away, you begin to give birth to a kind of *witness* who is able to observe without being identified with what it observes. This is the beginning of this process of intelligence, and it is one of the key principles of meditation.

My teacher liked to describe the spiritual path as "the sudden discovery of intelligence."[10] This sudden discovery of intelligence arises both in the practice of meditation and in life situations, especially when your schemes to secure yourself or control others suddenly fall apart.

This intelligence is experienced as moments of understanding or insight about how things are. You experience a sudden shift in perspective, recognizing that the way you saw a situation before was only partial, or even completely distorted. For a vivid moment, it's like waking up from a dream. These could be little glimpses. Over time they could become more and more powerful, reaching the level of "aha!" experiences, which all of us are familiar with.

It's your confidence in the truthfulness of these glimpses of how things are that keeps you moving forward on the path, because it's only through the sudden discoveries of intelligence that your relationship with hope and fear begins to change. As long as you are hypnotized by materialistic solutions, you are still engaged in your struggle with the mind of hope and fear. You block the functioning of that intelligence because while that mind is cunning, it is not intelligent. It's cunning in its ability to manipulate your world. The mind of hope and fear is not intelligent in the sense that it is ignoring the *space* that surrounds its project to keep things under control. *Space* means the open dimension of your life. It is the basic spaciousness that experiences arise and disappear within. This open dimension is always available to you in the present moment when you don't impulsively fill it with your schemes and strategies merely to avoid discomfort of any kind.

Intelligence, and the practice of identifying with nowness, invites you into this space, in which your strategies to control and manipulate the world fall apart over and over again. Amazingly, you begin to discover that even as the strategies fall apart, you are still here and you have more strength, rather than less.

This intelligence is also referred to as *penetrating insight.* It is penetrating because it is experienced directly, rather than filtered through the mind of hope and fear. While it tends to appear to you in a sudden way, gradually over time your confidence in its profound value develops, and the intelligence increases in frequency and power. It is this confidence that is crucial if you are to give birth to the living Buddha within you.

DEVELOPING CONFIDENCE IN WHAT YOU LEARN

In the Buddhist tradition, you slowly develop confidence by first studying the Dharma intellectually and then having a clear understanding of what has been taught. The word *Dharma* refers to the teachings of the Buddha about how to become free from confusion. It's a Sanskrit word that has been variously translated as "the way" or "the law of the universe" or "the truth of how things are." The Dharma taught by the Buddha developed in a culture that already had a long tradition of understanding this word in a different sense.

The dharma of Indian culture is the worldly or outer sphere of dharma. At its most basic, it simply refers to worldly things and worldly concerns altogether. At a more differentiated level, it refers to the appropriate or skillful way to conduct your affairs in any sphere of worldly life. Thus, we speak of the dharma of law, or of medicine, or of family life, or of cooking, or of marriage. Here the dharma refers to the right way to do things, usually according to long-established traditions.

By contrast, the Dharma of the Buddha is an inner or higher dharma. Like the lower dharmas of worldly life, it also refers to the appropriate or accurate or skillful way to conduct your life. But it is less concerned with conduct and more deeply concerned with insight and knowledge of your inner world, and with how to become a fully awakened human being.

By thinking about the Buddha's Dharma you have been taught—which you have studied and can chew on, digest, and apply to your life experience or abandon it if it isn't true for you—your confidence deepens and becomes more personal. But if you limit your connection with Dharma to the level of intellectual discourse alone, no matter how interesting and stimulating this may be, eventually your understanding of nowness will become merely a stale concept. You will edit the teachings in order to reassure your hopeful mind. The Dharma will then become another commodity to be sold to whomever wants to buy it.

The only safeguard is to practice meditation so that your understanding of what it means to identify with nowness is always fresh and up to date. In meditation, you drop the intellectual thinking and the logic and the concepts, and you just sit with nowness. By sitting like this, the deepest insight and intelligence arises, beyond words or theories or confusion. It is direct understanding, and this is the ultimate intelligence.

JOURNEYING GENUINELY
THROUGH MEDITATION

Because the materialistic mindset is extremely cunning and resourceful, it is ready to co-opt anything for its own agenda—including the Dharma. It tries to hijack the wisdom of the Buddha's approach by imitating it as closely as possible—like a fake Rolex. As a result, we often hear people speaking with great reverence about how they're really living in the present moment and that life has never been better. It is as if nowness were a fine wine and they have their own private reserve. Their focus is always on pleasurable experiences, never on challenging ones.

My teacher used to say to us again and again, "Without your practice, our real connection is extremely doubtful."

He also used to say that those who study Dharma without meditation are neurotic scholars, but those who meditate without study are dumb meditators. So you must bring together intellectual curiosity with brave and consistent dedication to facing your life directly in meditation practice. There does not seem to be any other way. Otherwise the Dharma will become corrupted, just as it did in other cultures in the past.

There is a parable about God and the Devil walking together: A diamond-like object is shining by the side of the road. God points to it and says, "Look—there's the truth!" And the devil says, "Wonderful—let's organize it!"

Because we are human, because we are materialistic, because we have hope and fear, and because we are looking for the easiest way out of our deep existential tension, we tend to corrupt things. That is why—especially in the beginning—awakening is a lonely path. But loneliness is a sign that you are moving in the right direction, because it means you have resisted the temptation to settle for the seductive imitations or shortcuts that can always be counted upon to draw a crowd.

It is up to each of us individually to carry the genuine Dharma forward by accessing the intelligence of penetrating insight through meditation. It is your tool on the journey of cutting through all the sources of corruption, both internal and external.

6

WHY PEOPLE MEDITATE

The vast majority of human beings who now share the earth with you have never made any kind of connection with meditation, and will never do so in this life. Even if they were exposed to Buddhist teaching and practice, they would not be the least bit interested. So why do people choose to meditate? They approach it with a range of motivations.

HAPPINESS

Everyone has the basic motivation to experience happiness in this life. Just like you.

Of course, there are innumerable versions of the path people follow to pursue happiness. We don't need to catalog or review them all, but essentially they would like to have what they want in order to assure not just survival, but also security—now and in the future. If their life includes some sort of religious belief, they might be good in this life to go to heaven after they die or to be reborn into a better circumstance than the one they are experiencing now. If they have come to the conclusion that this is the only life there is, then they would like to make it as good as possible, as comfortable as possible, as free of pain and inconvenience as possible—for themselves and for those near and dear to them.

We are all unconsciously embedded in the motivation to be happy because we are human. We hope for the best and fear the worst and take all that for granted.

The fact that you are being motivated and conditioned by hope and fear at every moment is something you accept. If Socrates were observing you, he would tell you that you are living an unexamined life, and that such a life is not worth living. Some people might tell Socrates to mind his own business. But if you do begin to examine your motivation in life even a little bit, you would still have the same basic attitude of wanting happiness for yourself and those near and dear to you, but you might also become curious about meditation. When you hear about meditation, you might feel that it's wholesome and that you want to be associated with it. You might conclude that practicing it could make you happier and your life better. In this sense, meditation becomes part of your hope. You think, *Perhaps if I practice meditation a little bit every day, my life will actually go better. It will help me relax, deal with my stress, be better organized, and work more efficiently. I'll be calmer, and people will like me more, and my family will find me easier to be around. Why not try it? It couldn't hurt!*

You see meditation more as an adornment to the life you already have. It's like a seasoning that will make things taste better.

This hope that meditation can make your life better is, in some sense, common to all levels of motivation. For most of us, there would be no reason to begin to meditate if we didn't have some faith it would have this result. We could call this a materialistic motivation, and we would be right, but this is not a reason to scorn or reject it out of hand.

At the next stage of motivation, you come to your interest in meditation because you've observed life more deeply—your own life, the lives of others you know, and even others you don't know. You're looking at a bigger picture.

RELIEF FROM SUFFERING

You notice that there is actually a great deal of suffering in the world and that your project of making yourself as happy and comfortable as possible is happening against this vast background of suffering. Some people seem to be very comfortable while others seem to be struggling a great deal. Some people have great good fortune, and others have a lot of misfortune and obstacles. Sadly, too, people are often not very kind to each other.

You also experience your own share of disappointment, of not always getting what you want, of undeniably getting older and perhaps having less zest for life, of your work or your children letting you down, and so on. You might ask yourself quietly, "Is this all there is?" At this point, you come to meditation a little less hopeful, a little more fearful or doubtful. You also start to ask many more questions, such as:

Why are things the way they are?

Why do I have this dissatisfaction, despite all my hopes and efforts and good intentions? Is there anything to be done about it?

Why do some people have so much and others so little?

Why is life so unfair?

Is there some justice—karmic or whatever—to how everything is unfolding?

Meditating a few minutes every day, even if you're able to sustain such an ambitious commitment, doesn't necessarily make all that dissatisfaction and anxiety go away, especially after the initial high of novelty wears off. All in all, you begin to suspect that practicing meditation only to make your day and your life go more smoothly might ultimately have little more effectiveness than changing the arrangement of the deck chairs on the Titanic.

AN ALLY IN DIFFICULTY

Then the motivation to meditate at this stage may well be that you see it as an ally in your aspiration to meet the inevitable difficulties of life with positive attributes, like courage and dignity.

With this motivation, you have no illusions; it is clear that the existential facts of sickness, old age, and death do apply to you and to everyone dear to you. Indeed, as you grow older, it takes considerable denial not to see this more and more clearly. You might even commit to meditation because you believe it can help you die well when death inevitably comes, whether you think there are future lives or not. Notice that hope and fear are still factors at this level, but they are grounded in a more sober view of life, stripped almost entirely of fantasy or wishful thinking.

FREEDOM FROM THE CAUSES OF SUFFERING

Beyond this level of motivation, the commitment to meditation is radical and sits in the very center of your life, all the time. Greater commitment is always the result of greater awareness and deeper examination of how things are. Such a commitment takes root when you conclude that suffering is an inevitable, universal, existential reality and that the aim of spiritual practice is to completely free yourself from the causes and conditions of this suffering, just as the Buddha himself did.

The Buddha called this basic state of suffering *samsara,* which means "spinning." Implicit in the meaning of this word is that we all create our own suffering moment after moment because of our compulsive habitual patterns of thought and behavior. We spin round and round in the same repetitive cycle of frustration. Only a deep and thorough uprooting of these habitual and painful distortions will really address the problem.

Very simply, at this point you are no longer trying to make samsara taste better. Meditation becomes a revolutionary gesture, with the aim to deconstruct the whole giant, futile edifice of hope and fear that keeps you trapped in the endless spin cycle of frustration and dissatisfaction.

TO BENEFIT OTHERS

The only commitment to the path of meditation beyond this comes when you no longer cherish the privacy of your own samsara or the importance of your own spiritual quest over anyone else's.

You find yourself reflecting, *If I am suffering, what about all the others?* If that inevitable tension between your endless wish to be happy and the inconvenient and limiting facts of your life is something everyone else also experiences, what should you do then? What must you do? Your motivation to meditate becomes based on this expansion of your vision and inspired by a sense of generosity.

To make the well-being of others as high a priority as your own—not just in occasional moments of crisis or heroism, but as a way of life—is as rare as a star in the daytime. When this is in fact the commitment, not only is there no longer any room for selfishness, but there isn't even any room for a self. We will examine this teaching on nonself much more deeply later. For now, suffice it to say that the Buddha taught that it is the source of all genuine happiness, courage, dignity, and power.

My teacher had a vision of a meditator as a warrior, whom he called the Shambhala Warrior—a heroic archetype arising out of the discipline of meditation who would speak to people universally, whatever their cultural background or core beliefs. The warrior is an archetype of gentleness and bravery rooted in courage, rather than the conventional warrior archetype of aggression and domination rooted in fear and cowardice. Especially in the secular world of the modern West, this archetype of the gentle but courageous warrior, who works tirelessly for others' benefit, has great power and resonance.[11]

THE MAP AND THE TERRITORY

Teachings like the ones in the previous chapter are merely maps that draw an outline of the path. Your actual day-to-day experience will always be much more fluid than any conceptual structure you might try to place it in. While the structure gives you a helpful map—especially in the beginning—once you begin to use the map, it leads you into the actual territory it describes. Inevitably you find that the territory is much richer, and much messier, than the map. It is not an obstacle to begin with the map, but your aim is to know the territory—to know the true meaning, and to know it from within.

THE MAP OF GREATER KNOWING

This particular map of motivational levels may seem to have a hierarchical quality, as if leading you to a particular conclusion and telling you that the final stage is obviously the best stage—the one you should be aiming for. But there isn't an underlying value judgment implied here about better or worse. It's more of an analysis about how your awareness can keep deepening and expanding.

The spiritual path is based on cultivating a certain kind of knowing. The whole journey is about that quality of knowing getting clearer, more open, and less self-centered. This is the key point: How much can you be aware of?

With this view, these levels of motivation are just a way of describing how a human being might naturally evolve her understanding. When you look at it purely as a linear process, it does feel as if you're being led to the conclusion that the final stage is the best. But if you see it more as a natural unfolding of awareness, like the layers of lotus petals peeling back and opening, then you can appreciate how you yourself might cycle through all the levels during your life, or even during a single day!

It's a big map of human possibilities. At times you may be living from the perspective of an early level, without feeling shame about it; at other times you really do taste the final level, without feeling proud about it.

For example, you practice for many years with the heartfelt vow that you're dedicating your life to others, but mainly you are practicing out of your ambition to be a perfect Buddhist. Eventually, you find that you can't sustain this approach because you have taken this vow of self-sacrifice at the cost of your own happiness. You give to others in ways that ignore your own needs. When you realize this, you feel such disillusionment that you give up the path altogether for a while, becoming a recovering Buddhist.

The gentle approach is to adopt a simpler and less ambitious attitude toward your practice. You might conclude that it is saner just to show up and honestly encounter whatever motivation you may be experiencing in the moment, without attaching so much lofty spiritual meaning to what you're doing. This is closer to the attitude of the journey without goal.

THE TERRITORY OF YOUR DAILY EXPERIENCE

As the levels of motivation cycle continuously throughout the day, you may find that you are actually hoping for something.

You're hoping that you're going to be a better person. You're hoping that you're not going to contribute to the chaos and the problems. When you're sitting in meditation, you're hoping the rest of the day is going to be calmer and you're going to feel better. When you go on retreat, you're hoping to come out more evolved so that you can help the world.

You could dismiss this hope as materialism. Certainly such attitudes can be forms of materialism, but you don't need to lay a heavy-handed value judgment on it. Your materialism is part of your human inheritance, and it isn't going away any time soon. Instead, it gives you a working basis for your journey.

Traditionally, we say that you are accepting your hopefulness and "bringing it to the path." What this means is that by experiencing things directly, you learn something you didn't know before, and you come to know it "in your bones"—not merely as someone else's idea or experience. Seeing how hopefulness motivates your practice is where your growth is happening, and you realize that *is* your path.

Simultaneously, your self-deception gets subtler, and the intelligence that sees this self-deception heightens. The point is that you're on an endless journey. If you take the attitude that the journey is about banishing all the negative things and strengthening all the positive things—to the point where you are absolutely perfect or invulnerable—then you've totally missed the point. That will never happen.

In fact, your hopes are part of the juice and the life force of your path. You are not going to find such good fuel anywhere else. So rejoice in your hopefulness, but also pay attention to the way in which you cling to your hope as a way of avoiding the experience of fear.

Because if you think the journey is about getting rid of the experience of fear, once and for all, again you are missing the point. The fear is always there, so cultivating a path that is trying to nurse only the hope is self-deception.

SPONTANEOUS ENCOUNTERS

There's a saying that you cannot solve any problem with the same mindset that created it. This is actually a beautiful description of the spiritual path. You have created your problems with the mind of hope and fear, and you will not solve them with hope and fear. Rather, you can work more fruitfully with these problems with the knowing or intelligence that can see your struggle from a different perspective. Engaging in this way is being without any attachment to the outcome.

Even though you see that your practice of dedicating your life to others' benefit still has a future-oriented and even an evangelical quality to it, in the deepest experience of the journey without goal you have let go of your sense of mission. There's only nowness. You are so fully identified with nowness, so devoid of hope and fear, that you no longer have any future. You act spontaneously in each moment, and then let go of the result.

In other words, there's nothing further to realize once you have exhausted your striving for a goal because you know with utter certainty that there was never anything but nowness and the endless suffering of all the others who haven't fully realized this. Of course, this is a very profound level of understanding, but it is worth appreciating as a measure of what is possible. My own teacher called this the practice of the master warrior.

If you have enough confidence in your knowing, then each encounter with others becomes a spontaneous expression of freeing yourself and them simultaneously, because there is nothing else going on for you. There are no longer any sidetracks from nowness.

PART TWO

MAKING FRIENDS
WITH YOUR MIND

THE PRACTICE THAT
BRINGS BRAVERY

The actual practice of working with hope and fear, the territory of your experience, begins to cultivate the intelligence that can connect you directly with the living Buddha within you. The practice that accomplishes this is *shamatha* meditation.

The Sanskrit word *shamatha* means "peaceful abiding." Sometimes it is translated as "cultivating peace" or "resting the mind" or simply "mindfulness." Whatever the translation, the same basic point is being conveyed. The underlying purpose of the practice is to develop a settled mind—a mind that is not easily agitated by external factors and is able to meet the challenges of life with some level of equanimity. This is a gradual, ongoing development.

The practice of shamatha meditation is not a specifically Buddhist practice, in fact its origin predates the life of the Buddha. During his lifetime, shamatha was practiced widely in the spiritual culture of India, and he learned it from other teachers. Almost all forms of meditation include some aspect of shamatha, so you can think of it as a kind of generic or universal practice that creates a foundation for all the others.

A FOUNDATIONAL TOOL
WITH PROFOUND EFFECTS

On one level, shamatha is not a particularly spiritual pursuit but a very ordinary and practical human pursuit. It is a somewhat mechanical practice in the sense that one of its main objectives is to help you develop an ability to rest the mind on a specific object of attention, such as the breath, a saying, or a visualization. It can have all kinds of useful applications, such as enabling you to become more focused and better able to handle the details of your daily life effectively. It can help you bring greater concentration and precision to all of your life's activities. For example, it can help you to accomplish a task that is as simple, but enjoyable, as making a cup of tea that is neither too weak nor too strong, but that is just right.

On a more spiritual level, learning how to rest the mind on an object of attention is the foundation for everything that comes afterward. The Buddha practiced variations of it for many years during his spiritual journey, before he discovered his own way of meditating and set off in his own direction. Depending on how you learn it, shamatha can become the platform for practices I described earlier that are based on *centralizing inwards,* or on *trying to become higher,* as well as on *becoming completely identified with nowness* as the Buddha advocated.

The Buddha could not have discovered enlightenment without first having being thoroughly trained in shamatha. This is a key point historically, and it also determines how the Dharma is taught and how it's practiced.

ALL-ENCOMPASSING PEACE

When we translate shamatha as "peaceful abiding," there is frequently a misunderstanding about what is implied by "peace." It is easy to think the purpose of shamatha is to create a cocoon of self-absorbed peacefulness while the chaos of the world is swirling all around you. Your peace is impenetrable, as if you are sitting in meditation in your apartment in midtown Manhattan and you no longer even hear the taxis honking their horns and the ambulances wailing their sirens. This may be the peace of *centralizing inwards,* but it is not the peace we want to cultivate through shamatha practice.

To cultivate the true, all-encompassing peace of shamatha, you remain open to the energy and chaos both within you and around you. To do this, you remain open in a very particular way—*not too tight, not too loose.*

Your practice is too tight when you are trying to fabricate, or force, an experience of peace by shutting out the liveliness of both your mental processes and the external world. It is too loose when the energy and chaos of your nowness overwhelms all your efforts to remain present and mindful, and instead it carries you away into distraction and confusion.

Shamatha is the practice by which you become familiar with the balance between too tight and too loose, and through this you learn how to ride the energy of the mind with a sense of stability. If you are going to become completely identified with nowness, then you have to be open to whatever arises: good or bad, happy or sad.

You can't pick and choose your preferred version of nowness. This is the pitfall of centralizing inwards. The peace of shamatha is not the peace of the cemetery where you "rest in peace." You are not learning how to be dead—actually you're learning how to be more alive. You are learning how to be as fully present and undistracted as possible with whatever arises.

Above all, you are learning to make friends with your mind. The discovery that you can fully accept yourself as you are is perhaps the single most powerful and transformative aspect of shamatha. It is the foundation—not only of the entire spiritual path—but of living a happy and fruitful life altogether.

VIEWING YOUR MIND AS A FRIEND

The philosopher Pascal said, "All of humanity's problems stem from man's inability to sit quietly in a room alone."[12] In the same way, all the problems of the world and all the unnecessary suffering in life begin because each of us, individually, is not able to make friends with our experience. Because of this, making friends with your mind is a very brave and even a heroic thing to do. The ultimate aim of your practice is to fully accept yourself as you are, and having this understanding gives you purpose and strength.

Holding this view is important especially as you begin your meditation practice, when you may not feel very strong or very motivated. If you remind yourself of your own friendliness every time you sit down, it's extremely helpful. Sitting in meditation is challenging, and if you are not able to remind yourself why you are doing it, again and again, you will eventually stop doing it.

EARLY CHALLENGES IN ESTABLISHING A PRACTICE

In the course of my own life as a Dharma student, teacher, and psychotherapist, I have seen many people give up on the practice of shamatha. I believe the reason this happens is because early on the deep and priceless value of the practice was not sufficiently imprinted. Particularly in the beginning, you will often experience your mind as very wild, and you may also experience a lot of physical discomfort. In my own case, both these reasons made the first few months of practicing shamatha quite difficult. I probably would have quit, but I learned it during a retreat, and there was peer pressure and support from the other meditators. I could feel that we were all riding our minds together, side by side, and this was a great encouragement.

The traditional word for being clear about why you're meditating is *view*. You have to have "the view." When you sit down to do any practice for the first time, you must be introduced to the view, otherwise you don't know what you're doing. As with any activity in your life, if you know why you're doing it, you will go toward it with greater enthusiasm and greater confidence.

It's important to distinguish the difference between having the view and having a goal, because we are still journeying without goal. Your goal is only your idea of the goal. The goal and your idea of the goal will never be the same. So the whole thing is an endless trap—you thought it might be like this, and then when you finally arrive, it turns out to be something entirely different and you fall into your habits of hoping for the best and fearing the worst. We might also say that having a goal is based on your ambition. Your ambition always involves a sense of poverty because you want to be somewhere other than where you are now or someone other than who you are now.

During the journey, you maintain the *view* because the view never gets old. The view is never wrong; the view will never lead you astray.

I am practicing shamatha to tame my distracted mind, to be fully present in my life, and to make friends with all my experiences. You cannot go wrong with that understanding because having the view is based more on aspiration than ambition. You begin with some kernel of faith that, as a human being, you are already basically good and that you have the potential to fully realize health and strength in your life. You have faith that you have a living Buddha within you and that you can fully realize that wakefulness, gentleness, and courage.

JOURNEYING THROUGH
PEACEFUL ABIDING PRACTICE

As you struggle with hope and fear along the way, holding the view of why you are practicing shamatha will help develop the clear person inside you who can see the fantasy involved with your hope and the strong person inside you who can stare the fear down. You slowly learn that you can outlast them both. You just sit through your fantasies and fears, and in sitting through them, you learn that they go away and you're still there. Then of course they come back again but not in quite the same way. Perhaps a certain construction of the hope and fear had you in its tight grip, and it is actually loosened, or even dissolved altogether.

Such experiences should not lead you to become complacent or to think that the journey is over because there will always be more on the path ahead. My teacher often said that the further the warrior goes, the more he or she embraces the challenge of hope and fear. He used the image of the samurai, walking down the street of the village, looking fiercely to left and right. He has already vanquished all the enemies on the street. But he looks down a dark alley off to the side, and says, "Oh, fantastic! Another dark alley where enemies might be lurking."

You might even develop a similar appetite for turning to face hope and fear. This happens when you have surrendered the goal—in this case the fantasy that your life is going to be some other way than it is—and you let making friends with your mind and relaxing with the endless display of hope and fear be your path.

THE ART OF MAKING
FRIENDS WITH YOURSELF

N ow let's look at how you actually practice shamatha. The instruction in shamatha meditation has three aspects to it. When you sit down to practice, it can be very helpful to begin by going through the three aspects of Body, Speech, and Mind in order, whether the session is ten minutes or an hour or whatever.

In meditation, Body, Speech, and Mind are called the Three Gates because all of the experiences you have in your life are going to come to you only through one of these three portals. The principle of Body is connected with the importance of your posture. Speech is connected with using your breath as the object of attention. Mind is connected with meeting whatever arises in your experience of nowness—whether it is your thoughts, emotions, feelings, bodily sensations, or sense perceptions.

So when you sit down to meditate, on either a meditation cushion or—if you find that uncomfortable or painful—a chair, it is very helpful to attune yourself first with Body, then with Speech, and then with Mind. Finally, you synchronize all three with each other and practice shamatha.

PREPARATION: REMEMBERING THE VIEW

Before we begin the instruction and the guided practice, bring to mind your motivation and your view as to why you are here, why you want to practice shamatha. Talk to yourself about the view out loud or silently. As you do this, remember that the meaning of the word shamatha is "peaceful abiding," remember the aspiration to be brave and gentle with your experience and to reaffirm your commitment to make friends with whatever arises.

CONNECTING WITH BODY

My teacher used to say that just taking the meditation posture can uplift your mind more than it was before. He encouraged us to notice that when people are depressed, their posture slouches. Just taking this posture, as described in the coming pages, can cheer you up! It's very powerful and very simple.

Having recalled the view, you relate to Body. To do this, close your eyes and have a sense of dropping down into your body, of gathering and collecting your physical energy. With your eyes closed, it is easier to cultivate the feeling that you are dropping down from your involvement with your thinking mind into the "mind" of the body, which pervades the body and is expressed as bodily sensations as well as an underlying feeling of the body.

Just sit with that, without any judgment about what you are experiencing. If there are places of tightness or pain or tension, simply extend a sense of kindness and relaxation to them.

Next, feel your connection with the earth, with the ground. Your body is an expression of this ground, and for that matter, the earth can be thought of as a gigantic body. Elementally it is no different than your own body.

In particular, feel that you have a good seat—that your buttocks are firmly on the cushion and your legs are comfortably crossed. It's as if you have formed a tripod of your buttocks and your knees. It is very stable, and it connects you firmly to the earth. Your hips should be higher than your knees so that there is no strain on your back. Depending on what is more comfortable for you, place the hands either with palms down on the thighs or with one hand cupping the other at the level of the abdomen. The arms should be loose and relaxed. If your hands are placed on the thighs, make sure they are not too far forward over your knees and not too far back toward your abdomen since both will put a slight strain on your back. Just let them rest very comfortably.

Remember the principle of uprightness, straightening the spine and the back. You can lift your shoulders slightly, exaggerate that and then let the shoulders drop and relax, while the spine remains straight. If you are sitting in a chair, sit upright, have your feet parallel to each other, firmly planted on the floor in front of you.

So straighten the posture, feel that connection with the earth, and then *relax!*

Systematically relax various areas of the body. Relax the muscles around your heart and your belly; let them be very open and soft. Relax your shoulders. Relax the muscles of the face and the jaw by parting your lips very slightly as if you are about to say "Ahhh" and placing your tongue on the roof of your mouth behind the front teeth. Finally, tuck the chin in ever so slightly so that there is a slight curve at the top of the straight spine.

Take a moment to fully feel this posture. *Grounded . . . upright . . . relaxed.*

CONNECTING WITH SPEECH

Now we turn to the principle of Speech. Speech here refers to the breath because breath is the basis of speech and the voice, of any sound you make. Breath is also the living, energetic connection between the body and the mind. The word *yoga*, which means "union," refers to this joining of body and mind through the vehicle of the breath. So breath is very important in meditation practice and has been for several thousand years. As an object of mindfulness, the breath has several wonderful qualities. First, it is always with you, as long as you are alive. Second, it links you directly to nowness. Third, it is inherently gentle and soothing.

The instruction for practicing shamatha is this: *Place your attention on the movement of your breath as it goes in and out of your body.*

Let the eyes remain closed. Notice now that your breath is a moving bodily sensation, and place your mind on it. Place your attention on your breath as it moves through wherever you experience it in your body: Maybe in your abdomen, maybe in the chest at the level of the heart, maybe in your throat, your nostrils, or your lips. Maybe you experience it in all these places. Let your attention rest on the feeling, wherever it is.

It is important to tune into the sensation of the breath, rather than locking tightly onto it. Don't try to sustain a continuous experience; as there will be little highlights of sensation, there will be little gaps where the sensation is not prominent or is even altogether absent. Just go along with it, with a light touch.

Remember, you're not using the breath to centralize inwards, nor to induce a state of trance—you're using it to identify with nowness. To help do this, flash on your posture now and then. Feel your connection with the ground, gently straighten your spine and relax your shoulders. If there's tightness in the jaw or the face or in the area of the heart or the belly, just be aware of that and relax. Just let it relax. Your connection with body will support your connection with nowness.

For the first time, gently open your eyes. Because the chin is tucked in slightly, your eye gaze naturally falls downward, three to four feet in front of you. With the eyes open, we now move into the instructions for working with Mind, the third of the Three Gates.

CONNECTING WITH MIND

The connection between the eye gaze and the mind is very important. In shamatha meditation, the eye gaze is soft and diffused and relaxed. The reason the gaze is soft is because you're using the eyes to look at the mind, not to look out at objects.

Obviously, if your eyes are open, you are going to see the visual field, but don't focus on it. Your eyes don't grasp at what they see the way they usually do. You're not looking for any feedback from what you see.

Instead, you're looking inward, directly at the mind. "Mind," in this case, is all the activities of which your mind is capable and which you can experience in nowness: your thoughts, your emotions, your feelings, your bodily sensations, and your perceptions from the five senses. Whatever arises in nowness that can be known in any way is "mind."

Once again, flash your attention on your posture. Adjust it slightly if you need to; flash on your connection with the earth; make sure that the back and spine are straight, that the front of your body is open and relaxed; and continue to place the mind on the movement of the breath—in and out.

Then include the instruction for working with your mind, which is this: *Whatever occurs, neither suppress it as it arises nor follow it once it appears.*

Another way of saying this is that you should neither block the thoughts at the beginning nor chase them at the end. The instruction not to suppress is important because it cuts through any misconception you might have that meditation is about forcefully stopping thoughts or emptying the mind. Thoughts themselves are not regarded as an obstacle. You do not stop their flow in shamatha practice. You *never* stop their flow. For periods of time the flow will stop on its own. This is fine, and pleasurable, but you do not attach any special importance to this experience of stillness.

Thoughts are not the problem. Only your habitual tendency to identify with the thoughts, fixate on them, and be distracted by them is the problem. This tendency is addressed by the second part of the instruction: not to follow the thought once it appears.

Once again, we are practicing the art of *not too tight, not too loose.* This balanced approach is a thread that runs through all the practices and all the teachings we will be exploring. When working with thoughts, this balanced approach means that we respect the energy of our mind in each moment of meditation, but we don't let our fascination with the content of our thought process hijack our ability to remain present with whatever is happening.

A helpful metaphor is that practicing shamatha is like sitting at ease on the grassy bank of a stream. The stream is flowing endlessly. All kinds of debris pass by in the current of the stream: leaves, branches, old orange peels, soda cans—flotsam and jetsam of all kinds. Sitting there, you just let it flow and observe what passes without moving from your comfortable seat on the bank. In the same way, sit in meditation and observe thoughts, feelings, and sensations flowing through your experience.

There will come a moment when you realize you jumped in the stream and that as you paddled after something that was flowing by, you were swept downstream. In other words, you were absorbed in a thought, and for a while it thoroughly distracted your mind.

Here's the magic of meditation: The moment you realize what has happened, you don't have to laboriously pull yourself out of the water—you're immediately sitting back on the bank again! Then you simply continue the practice by flashing on your good posture, tuning into the sensation of the breath, and observing your mind without blocking or chasing what arises in nowness.

THE EFFECTS OF PRACTICING
THE INSTRUCTIONS

Shamatha develops your capacity to know that your thoughts, feelings, emotions, bodily sensations, and sense perceptions are occurring at the moment they're occurring and to be able to distinguish them from one another in nowness. The mind of shamatha knows *a thought is happening now* or *oh, strong anger is happening now!* or *the sound of that bird call is happening now.* It's almost like a clerk at a checkout counter with a very mechanical quality to the knowing.

At the same time, this knowing can only happen if you're not distracted by what's happening in your mind in the present moment. And being undistracted in that way is no small accomplishment! When you practice shamatha, you are training yourself to *dis-identify* with your thoughts, emotions, and so on. In doing this, you create the *witnessing* mind, which you begin to identify with, rather than the thoughts themselves. That mind is the first stage of knowing.

To create, or strengthen, that witnessing mind, we give it an object of attention—something it can keep coming back to that's neutral, such as the breath. In shamatha, we call this an *object of virtue.*

Virtue here doesn't mean that it's holy, particularly, or that your thoughts are profane. It simply means that bringing your attention back to it will not create any further mischief in the form of neurosis. For a long time— countless lifetimes, according to the Tibetans—you have been familiarizing yourself with your confused thoughts and emotions, which have created pain for you. The general word for meditation in Tibetan is *gom,* which means "to become familiar with." So far, for much of your life, you have been meditating only on your neurosis.

In the practice of shamatha, you are instead becoming familiar with the breath as an object of attention. Why not familiarize yourself with something helpful, rather than something harmful? If you really understand the truth of this, you will dedicate yourself to meditation, and you will learn what *peaceful abiding* means, firsthand.

But that is just the beginning of the process of knowing, which keeps going deeper as you journey along. Continuously deepening and refining this capacity to know is the basis of the whole spiritual path.

CLARIFYING QUESTIONS ABOUT PEACEFUL ABIDING PRACTICE

Should I practice shamatha every day?

In my experience, any prescription about how often you should meditate will more than likely set you up for failure. Of course it would be optimal if you could sit each day, especially in the beginning. But more important is the quality of your practice when you sit down to do it. You do it wholeheartedly. You give it 100 percent.

You will be much more likely to be wholehearted with any practice you do if you remind yourself why you are doing it in the first place. You have to look again and again at your motivation. You may be doing it because you feel you're a bad person if you don't. You tell yourself: *I was told to do this once, and I did it a couple of years ago, and it was kind of nice, but I don't really have time for this. And why am I doing it again? I just can't seem to get into it. I'm just no good.*

That kind of attitude is obviously not so helpful. Whereas if every time you sit down, you start with what the Zen master Shunryu Suzuki Roshi called "beginner's mind"—an attitude of openness and curiosity such as a child might have—you may be more willing to keep at it.

Just begin again and again, remembering the view: *Oh yes, here I am again on my meditation cushion. I vow to tame this distracted mind and to make friends with whatever arises. I'm going to do this on the cushion so that I can do it in my life because that's where it really matters.* It's okay to talk to yourself like this, even saying it out loud—but do it before you start to practice, not while you're practicing.

Now, if you take the attitude that you're going to practice because then you'll be a great meditation master someday, you're missing the point altogether. You're going to do this on the cushion so you can do it in your life. No one cares what a great hope-and-fear-conqueror you are on your cushion.

So it really doesn't matter so much whether you do it every day. What matters is that when you do it, you really do it. And each time you really do it, you're going to have more of an appetite to do it again because you are going to feel the clear difference between a life of distraction and a life of mindfulness. You'll feel that contrast, and you'll know that it matters.

How do I practice at those times when the view isn't clear or I can't really connect with it in a heartfelt way? What do I do when the only response I can find sounds something like, "Do I have to?"

Sometimes the view will be very clear for you. You will feel tremendous appreciation, and the inspiration to practice will be almost effortless. Other times, it will be more obscure, and while you may try to force yourself to sit, it feels aggressive. The fact that the quality of your motivation changes from time to time is just a message that your longing and your resistance are still of equal strength. In some ways *the whole path is an endless back and forth between your longing and your resistance.* In fact, this is how you're bringing hope and fear to the whole "project" of meditation altogether.

Sometimes your longing will be very strong and you will feel hopeful about your practice. At other times your resistance is stronger, and it's as if you have to push through a vague sense of dread to reach the cushion. Rather than waiting for your inspiration to strike, right there you can experience an appreciation for how the hope and the fear are operating and how fickle they are, and just go right into that experience. And if every once in a while you go to the cushion only because you feel you should, that's not a problem! Just do it. The moment you step over your resistance, something shifts. Always. Every time.

Is there a presumption that when we sit, hope and fear will soon come visit us? What if they don't?

Wait a little longer.

In other words, you can't be too obsessive about making this connection, assuming that every time you sit down, along will come hope and along will come fear. If you sit a lot, sometimes your meditation will be very peaceful, in the sense that your mind will be still, with very few thoughts. Then you may have a tendency to cling to that experience or feel that it's an accomplishment—which is of course an expression of your hope about meditation. When you do this, you inevitably set yourself up for disappointment.

The main issue here has to do with understanding the larger background, which is that hope and fear are deeply ingrained in each of us and that if we sit down regularly and open ourselves up, they will inevitably come along. Even if they appear to be dormant, we have an understanding that at the deepest level, this is what we're working with because we are human beings.

If there's pain or discomfort in my posture, should I regard it as a distraction that I can ignore and inwardly accommodate, or should I respond to it and outwardly address it?

There is a fine line to consider between those two responses. Just knowing that there is a line is really the key point. Exactly where your line falls is a very personal thing. My teacher addressed that question by encouraging us to distinguish between physical pain and psychosomatic pain.

Physical pain tends to be simple and straightforward. When it is just physical pain and it interferes with your ability to hold your mind to the breath, you should adjust your posture.

Psychosomatic pain, on the other hand, will arise in the body as a sublimation of psychological material that's not being dealt with. You become distracted by that pain and preoccupied with it as a way of actually blocking the arising of other painful material in the mind. And when it is on that level, if you are able to identify it as such, it's very important that you stay with it until the painful bodily sensations begin to relax and the other material begins to come up.

That is the rule of thumb, but it's a very personal matter. The most important rule is that you should not unnecessarily torment yourself when you're sitting. In one of his earliest instructions, my teacher said that the most important thing when you meditate is to be physically comfortable. So it is better to sit on a chair and be comfortable than to sit on a cushion and be uncomfortable. But beyond that general guideline, navigating pain during practice is very much up to you. Over time you gain such familiarity with your own patterns that you begin to know how to handle the different types of pain that arise.

If meditating with eyes closed is more comfortable, why must I meditate with eyes open?

Keeping the eyes closed encourages a dreamy mental state and a tendency to create a cocoon by withdrawing into yourself. Having closed eyes is helpful when you begin a session because doing so enables you to collect yourself and drop down into your bodily experience. But after that initial grounding, it's more important to encourage a precise, wakeful state that is tuned into the present moment. You stay tuned into knowing what's happening *now*. When you're fully awake, your eyes are open. It's very simple.

SYNCHRONIZING THE
BODY AND THE MIND

Unlike the Western philosophical tradition, which views mind and body as two separate things, the Buddha taught that mind and body are interconnected and inseparable. The French philosopher Descartes established a foundation of dualism in thinking about how we experience things when he wrote that the observer and what was being observed were two separate yet equally independent realities.

The Buddha, on the other hand, never considered the body as separate from the mind. For the Buddha, and for the traditions that arose from his discoveries, a body separate from the mind is merely a corpse. So the body is alive, and what it is alive with is the mind.

The mind is the governing principle from which everything else emerges. Therefore, as the Buddha put it, "The mind is the king of all dharmas."[13] The body provides the necessary seat, or ground, for the mind to function. When the Buddha's close disciple Ananda was practicing extreme asceticism in his meditation, almost to the point of starving himself, the Buddha told him (remembering his own experience years earlier!):

Ananda, if there is no food there is no body. If there is no body, there is no dharma. If there is no dharma, there is no enlightenment. Therefore go back and eat.[14]

Within your own meditation practice of mindfulness, one of the discoveries you will make is that the relationship between your mind and body is not that clear. It is somewhat distorted and complicated. Your mind has many ideas and concepts about your body. This overly complicated version of the body is sometimes called the *psychosomatic body*, which is based on the assumption of dualistic separation, "I have a body" rather than "I am a body." My teacher distinguished this body created out of your thoughts from what he called the "real body" or the "body-body."[15]

To emphasize the difference between the two, consider the difference between eating when you're hungry and eating simply because it's lunchtime whether you're hungry or not. The first is an activity in which you relate to the real body and its real needs, in real time. The second is an example of your tendency to relate to your expectations about the body: that you should eat at lunchtime because you always eat at lunchtime. The first is grounded directly in your present experience, while the second is merely an expression of your conditioning, which you often respond to unconsciously and automatically, without paying attention to the reality of your immediate situation.

This example shows how strong and persuasive your habitual patterns of thought and action are. Your psychosomatic body is perpetuated and strengthened by the continuous flow and compelling logic of your thoughts.

A traditional Zen anecdote conveys the importance of cutting through your illusions of the psychosomatic body to the grounded reality of your body-body. When a student asks the master, "How can I practice in order to attain enlightenment?" the master replies, "When hungry, eat; when tired, sleep."

EXPERIENCES OF THE PSYCHOSOMATIC BODY

In my work as a psychotherapist, I see this identification with the psychosomatic body, and its destructive effects on my clients' sense of well-being, play out in a variety of ways—some of which you may find very familiar. Of course, you may object that the generalities that follow are stereotyping men and women. Obviously, not all my clients fall into these divisions. But I make them in service of a point about cultural stereotypes that we do take on individually.

When experiencing anxiety—about a job interview, for example—you find yourself in the grip of your conditioned, psychosomatic body. At such times your compulsive identification with your thoughts creates tremendous tension in the body, which usually happens outside your awareness. You may even lose your sense of connection with the body altogether because you are unconsciously trapped in the speed or fear of a particular mental state. This feeling of disconnection may be experienced in the following ways.

Among many of my male clients, it seems to play out in workaholic tendencies, fueled by the anxiety that if they don't continue to move as quickly as they can on whatever treadmill of livelihood they are currently running on, they will fail. For my male clients, this failure is feared almost as much as dying. In the process of avoiding it, many will compromise and even sacrifice their health to stress. The body-body is buried in a mirage of future expectations, which flickers back and forth between the hope for ultimate success and the fear of ultimate failure.

Among some of my female clients, it seems to manifest in shame about body image measured against cultural ideals of beauty, and the compulsive and addictive patterns—such as eating disorders—that they use in order to cope with their belief that they are not basically good and whole just as they are.

Even a moment's reflection about each of these syndromes takes us to a deeper consideration of the larger, destructive cultural influences and stereotypes that drive this suffering for men and for women. This is the sad consequence of a materialistic worldview, which creates an endlessly receding mirage of perfection and success that not even the most "perfect" and "successful" people can hope to reach, much less sustain. As for "ordinary" people, they can only watch this grand but punishing game of chasing illusion from the sidelines.

The deeper point is that we are all being driven by standards and expectations that we never asked for. They are socially and culturally determined, and we simply take them on, as if we had absolutely no choice, because that's what the world says is "real." We come up with criteria for success and failure based on these standards that become deadly serious for us. Our very lives depend on them, and individuals sometimes even kill themselves for not measuring up.

Any kind of mindful attention is quite difficult to sustain in the midst of the neurotic speed and stressful lifestyle of our society. The ceaseless subliminal message of our way of life is that we must keep moving, consuming, producing, and finding novelty. We have created a world of endlessly proliferating artificial wants, which conceal and override our simple, elemental *needs*. This neurotic speedy energy, which pulsates all around us, makes it challenging just to *be*. As it has been said, we have become human *doings* instead of human beings. Meditation gives us the opportunity to step back and ask ourselves, how real *is* all that?" and to ask this every day. It's a powerful way to live.

USING BODY AWARENESS TO TAME THE MIND

Your body is the place where a sense of beingness is first experienced. The practice of meditation facilitates the challenging process of unlearning this conditioned relationship with your body, and making contact with—even accepting and celebrating—your body as it actually is. This real body is the one that keeps giving you the message that you exist in the present moment, only in the present moment, and choicelessly in the present moment.

My teacher introduced me to the five senses as gateways to deeper wakefulness, in which the ordinary world is perceived as an inherently sacred place.

The five senses are the link between your body and the environment. But fueled by your anxiety, you usually speed past these sacred gateways. You rarely slow down enough to truly look at things, listen to things, smell, taste, or touch things. This speed is invariably the expression of anxiety, or of what my teacher referred to as "the fearful mind." Thus you miss the real juice and the real marrow of life in the present moment.

Appreciating your existence as a body-body can slow the neurotic speed of the psychosomatic body. The best way for your mind to begin to slow down enough that it can truly connect with your body is, first, to take the stable, uplifted, relaxed posture of shamatha practice. Then your mind can begin to pick up on your body's simple message of groundedness and ease.

THE POWER OF THE MEDITATIVE POSTURE

Limitations of language may give the misleading impression that your mind and body are separate. But that is not the case. The best that our language can convey here is that your body and mind are two inseparable aspects of a unified field of experience. Teachers in the Zen tradition cut through the limitations of language with poetic simplicity when they issue this gentle command to students who want to go beyond words to real experience:

"Just sit."

When you "just sit," you automatically experience a shift in your relationship with your thoughts and with the body created by these thoughts. You slowly disengage from the momentum of your psychosomatic hopes and fears. You land fully in nowness for the first time, even if only for a fleeting moment. As my teacher put it, you discover that "your thoughts have a flat bottom."

Another way of saying this is that your mind and body begin to synchronize. This phrase, "synchronizing mind and body," is used to describe one of the accomplishments of Shambhala warriorship. In fact, it is said to be a necessary foundation for the warrior's path altogether. In order to do anything properly and to relate to the details of your daily life with any kind of precision or skill, your body and mind must be synchronized. And the breath is a major gateway to accomplishing this.

USING THE BREATH TO SYNCHRONIZE

As in the instruction for practicing shamatha, the breath is the connecting principle that joins mind and body. We can visualize that the breath is physically located midway between mind and body as it enters through orifices in the head and descends into the chest. The breath resembles the body in its tangibility, in that we can feel it. It resembles the mind in its movement, or what we might call its fickleness, because we can't really grasp or hold onto it. It is subtler than the body and grosser than the mind.

In the Tibetan tradition, it is taught that the mind actually rides on what are called the "inner winds" of the body. When these are disturbed, they generate neurotic mental states—such as depression, anxiety, and irritability—that can be precisely identified and correlated with the disturbances. This understanding of the inner winds is one of the foundations for Tibetan medical diagnosis. The "outer" breath that you experience, and that you make use of as an object of mindfulness in shamatha meditation practice, is actually a coarse version of these subtle, inner winds. The quality of its movement affects these winds, which in turn affect the quality of your mental and emotional experience. When you bring the mind back to the breath, the breath is an anchor for the mind—which is subtler than using the body as an anchor, but equally useful in strengthening mindfulness.

As I discussed earlier in the basic instruction for shamatha practice, your attention to posture and breath is the starting point. You begin with an upright yet relaxed posture, described memorably by my teacher as "strong back, soft front." Then you place your attention on the natural movement of your breath as it passes in and out of your body.

As you meditate in this way, your attention on the posture and the breath make them into a connecting principle, a bridge, between the body's groundedness and the mind's openness.

12

FEAR, COWARDICE, BRAVERY, AND FEARLESSNESS

The Tibetan word for a male warrior is *pawo* and for a female warrior is *pamo*. They mean "the one who is brave." This definition reminds us once more that being a warrior in the Shambhala tradition has nothing to do with war or aggression, but is connected instead with courage. One thinks of a similar term for warriors in the Native American culture: braves.

BEING WITH FEAR

There is a saying from the Shambhala teachings: "Without knowing the nature of fear, it is impossible to discover fearlessness."[16] This tells us that the warrior's bravery develops out of his or her willingness to look directly at the experience of fear to learn what that experience really consists of. Without that willingness there is no way to be fearless.

In the Shambhala teachings and on the path to waking up, fear is regarded as a tremendously positive experience. Your very capacity to wake up fully is closely connected with your capacity to experience fear without turning away from its sharp and penetrating energy. Fearlessness does not mean "being without fear," which is more an expression of insensitivity, even stupidity, than it is an expression of warriorship. Popular culture celebrates the stereotype of the invincible male warrior armed with swords, guns, or bombs, conquering and destroying everything in his path. That is more of an adolescent, macho pretense and is beside the point here.

What fearlessness really means is being fully with fear, going through the fear, going beyond the fear. Therefore, fear itself is never the obstacle to fearlessness, but the entry point.

The key to being able to practice and live in this way is gentleness. Chögyam Trungpa taught that gentleness is indispensable to the experience of genuine warriorship and symbolized this quality with an open fan. In wedding ceremonies that he created and conducted for his Shambhala students, the bride would present a fan to the groom, which she would open as she offered it to him. The fully unfolded fan powerfully evokes the sense of openness and spaciousness that is inherent to the mind of meditation. It reminds us of the peace we cultivate in shamatha practice, which allows the energy of thoughts and emotions to arise in open space without suppressing or blocking anything.

DENYING FEAR

Because fear is such a key steppingstone on your path to fearlessness, the most formidable obstacle on your path is not fear, but rather your unwillingness to relate to fear and to face it directly. The moment you invest in that unwillingness and begin to build your life around it is the moment you turn away from warriorship.

Turning away like this is not merely an individual endeavor. Entire societies and cultures, with their political and economic systems, can, have, and generally do turn away from warriorship in this way. The most descriptive word for this turning away is *cowardice*. Cowardice is the antithesis of warriorship. It means—not that you are fearful—but that you have made yourself an expert in refusing to examine your fear when it appears. You do this because confronting the sharp energy of fear is uncomfortable and unpleasant. Out of a refusal to face such discomfort, you create a bubble of denial and self-deception.

In one of the most famous moments in Shakespearean drama, Julius Caesar's wife Calpurnia tells him of her previous night's dream in which she saw him dead at the hands of his colleagues in the Roman Senate. She urges him not to go to the Senate that day. In response to her, he says:

> Cowards die many times before their deaths.
> The valiant never taste of death but once.
> Of all the wonders that I yet have heard
> It seems to me most strange that men should fear,
> Seeing that death, a necessary end,
> Will come when it will come.[17]

It would be easy to be cynical about this speech and take the point of view that for Caesar, "discretion" would have been "the better part of valor" or that his pride and feelings of invulnerability proved to be his undoing. Yet Caesar's words here do have enduring power. In the context of the teachings of warriorship, his speech could be seen as commentary on the prison of living a life based on hope and fear. When your life is always conditioned by hope and fear, you are unable to fully live. When you shrink from the directness of life, you die many times before your death. You look for comfort above all else. You repeatedly take shelter in safe, predictable routines, hoping they will protect you from the unexpected. But ultimately these habits of avoidance only steal your vitality and creativity. This is a kind of death in life because life's energy is no longer fully available to you.

THE COCOON OF COWARDICE

In the Shambhala tradition, the experience of this psychological prison is called the *cocoon*. This term requires some explanation because we tend to think of the cocoon in positive ways, as a place of transformation and an alchemical laboratory in which the caterpillar is transmuted into the butterfly. But in the teachings of warriorship, the cocoon is not an inherently creative situation. Rather it is a stagnant situation.

The cocoon is a kind of casing that has slowly grown and surrounded you. It has been woven—thread by thread—by habits like your addiction to comfort, or to keeping busy, or to entertaining yourself whenever the possibility of an open moment presents itself to you. You think the walls, layers, and filters are protecting you, but in fact they stand between you and the raw exhilaration of being alive. As a result of this casing, you become numb, asleep to what is going on around you.

Over years of observing and practicing with their own cocoons, Shambhala warriors have come up with many metaphors for how it works. Here are some helpful ones:

- The cocoon feels as if your fear has backed up, the way plumbing sometimes gets backed up in an old house. There's a stale, stuck quality.

- Seeing your cocoon is like walking into a room that's empty but where people have been smoking and drinking and have left their mess of overflowing ashtrays and glasses with flat beer pooled in the bottom.

- Feeling your cocoon is like listening to Muzak in the elevator. Whom do they play that for? Hearing it brings feelings of sadness and listlessness, and at the same time, a sense that you're being lulled into a twilight zone where you no longer have to feel anything raw or genuine. It induces a kind of emotional anesthesia.

- Like plastic flowers in a hotel lobby, the cocoon never dies because it was never alive to begin with.

TRUE AND FALSE FEAR

This is the world of the cocoon. Perhaps the most succinct definition for the cocoon in this sense is that it is "a body of unexamined fear." Distinguishing between *true fear* and *false fear* gives us further insight into how the cocoon is formed and maintained. True fear is the direct experience of something that is threatening your existence, here and now. Perhaps you step out onto the avenue without noticing that a car is coming toward you very fast. The moment of noticing it is a moment of genuine fear. It wakes you up abruptly, and you feel the rush of adrenalin. It demands your attention and your immediate response. You get out of the way quickly because your very survival is at stake and there is no other option but self-destruction. This is very simple and straightforward. It is a dramatically wakeful experience.

False fear, on the other hand, is your anxiety about what has not yet happened, and in fact may never happen. You have not met the imagined or anticipated threat in real time. It is in speculative, future time. You worry. You chew anxiously on the possibility of negative consequences. This discursive worry robs you of your capacity to be fully present with your life. This is the fear of Caesar's coward, who dies many times before his death. This is the fear with which you weave the walls of your cocoon, thread by thread.

When you practice shamatha, you are engaging the false fear of the cocoon and the whole environment of repetitive thoughts and reactive emotions that it produces. You are dealing with its old, stale storylines and its predictable strategies. You are simply being with it and seeing it clearly, perhaps for the first time.

The false fear can only survive on your willingness to believe its messages. In the practice of shamatha, you withdraw your support for that tired but tenacious project. You provide a container in which it can play itself out until it runs out of gas, so to speak.

You also begin to realize that what you are witnessing as you sit on the cushion is what actually runs your life off the cushion. The false fear and its habitual patterns of thought and emotion affect your actions in the world and all of your relationships with other people, down to the smallest interaction. Its power comes solely from the fact that you are unaware of this.

In some sense this is a rude awakening. The presence of the cocoon is an overwhelming discovery, and a common reaction is for you to be hard on yourself about what you're seeing, and even want to reject these parts of yourself altogether.

CLARITY AND GENTLENESS

To return to Shambhala wedding symbolism, the bride gives the groom an open fan, and in turn the groom presents a ceremonial sword to the bride. The sword remains in its scabbard because its power is implied and does not need to be actively demonstrated. The sword here symbolizes the clarity and sharpness of the meditative state. It is the aspect of the witnessing mind that is able to cut through confusion and deception to reveal the truth of what is there.

The clarity and sharpness of this knowing faculty that we all possess is what exposes the cocoon for what it really is. Each time you let go of your habit of clinging to a habitual train of thought in shamatha practice, you allow the sword to effortlessly perform its function.

It is also this witnessing aspect of shamatha that most requires gentleness toward yourself because it is only through gentleness that you can truly make peace with such a powerful opponent as the cocoon. The key to practicing gentleness is to give up the ambition to rid yourself of those parts of yourself that displease you because this ambition is just based on further aggression toward yourself, and in the long run it only heightens and prolongs your struggle.

Spiritual practice is not a self-improvement project. Rather, it is about developing a friendly—and even a loving—attitude toward your cocoon. You realize how long and how deeply you believed you could not live without it. You let go of it with kindness, one thread at a time.

You allow your mind to take on the characteristics of an open fan: a gentle, spacious attitude that you cultivate as a warrior on your endless journey of making friends with your experience. As the poet Rainer Maria Rilke wrote:

> Perhaps all the dragons in our lives are princesses who
> are only waiting to see us act, just once, with beauty and
> courage. Perhaps everything that frightens us is, in its
> deepest essence, something helpless that wants our love.[18]

THE ROOTS OF OUR ANXIETY

All materialism begins with the fundamental instinct to survive. This instinct, and the possibility that you will not survive, is always present in life. There is no way to get rid of this. Nor can you grow out of the fear that comes with this awareness. It's not as if you are now an adult who can look back upon your childish fears with understanding and humor. It's not even something you can dispel with comforting words and objects, as you offer to comfort your children when their fears threaten to overwhelm them.

This anxiety about existence itself remains. As the poet W. H. Auden wrote when Nazi aggression threatened all of Europe in 1939, in some sense we human beings are always "children afraid of the night, who have never been happy or good."[19]

SOURCES OF ANXIETY IN WESTERN PSYCHOLOGICAL THEORY

An underlying theme in the Western psychological tradition that began with Freud is a passionate curiosity about the sources of our anxiety. Freud's willingness to explore anxiety deeply by means of scientific investigation rather than as a purely literary intuition was a revolutionary moment in Western intellectual history. For the first time, psychology became a scientific pursuit. Freud legitimized it.

For Freud, anxiety had different sources depending on which of three kinds of anxiety you were experiencing: "normal," "neurotic," or "moral."

- Normal anxiety originated in the struggle of the *ego*—the conscious, managerial function of the mind—to cope with the ongoing challenges of life.

- Neurotic anxiety originated as a conflict between the wishes of the *unconscious*—mainly focused either on sexuality or aggression—and the attempts of the ego to control those wishes.

- Moral anxiety originated as a conflict between the ego (that poor, besieged ego!) with the *superego*—the aspect of our psyche that is hemmed in by social hang-ups, taboos and norms, and "shoulds" of all kinds.

Many psychological thinkers who followed Freud challenged his conclusions, as happens in the evolution of any scientific theory. One of these challenges is of particular interest when considering meditation and the teachings of the Buddha.

The existential psychologists—influenced directly by the earlier European existential philosophers, especially Nietzsche—did not flatly deny the sources of anxiety identified by Freud, but asserted that anxiety had deeper roots. To give a sense of the uncompromising depth these philosophers brought to their view of anxiety, here is a quote from the theologian Paul Tillich. In it, he draws a distinction between the neurotic anxiety that Freud had named, and a deeper kind:

(Unlike neurotic anxiety,) ontological anxiety is nothing other than your awareness that you are finite. You become aware of it at certain moments. Though you are not always anxious, anxiety is always there, just as non-being and finitude are always there. It is exceedingly important that you affirm and not deny this anxiety. Nothing is more dangerous, even politically dangerous, than to believe you can avoid it by turning away from it.[20]

FOUR ULTIMATE CONCERNS

Based on influences such as this, the American psychologists Rollo May and Irvin Yalom pointed to what they called "ultimate concerns" that all human beings must deal with in the course of life. These ultimate concerns, according to their view, are the real roots of our anxiety. These concerns are

- the certainty of death,
- the truth of aloneness and the possibility that we may never discover the love that can make this aloneness bearable, and
- the need to create meaning in our lives and the possibility that we will fail to do so in a way that leads to despair.

They identify a fourth concern, perhaps slightly less immediate than the first three, but to which the Buddha would certainly have nodded his agreement. They call this "the burden of freedom," the radical and open-ended freedom to make of our lives what we will, and the courage required to navigate this open-endedness.[21]

NONTHEISM: WEST AND EAST

The existentialists argue that this freedom emerges as an ultimate concern for human beings when they stop believing in God or if they have never believed in God. Without this belief and the security and comfort of a Divine Plan, we experience that we are truly alone in the universe, left to make of life whatever meaning we can.

In the West, this sense that "God is dead" (to draw from Nietzsche) has had huge ramifications. But for the Buddha, this realization is part of a very old story. He himself lived through it twenty-five hundred years ago, when he abandoned the Indian theistic cultural and spiritual assumptions he was born within in order to discover his own path, embracing the existential burden of freedom fearlessly.

This path led him to the conclusion that the existence of a Divine Being is finally unknowable and that human beings must resolve their condition of anxiety and suffering for themselves. My own teacher, Chögyam Trungpa, often referred to the truth of suffering as "existential anxiety," bringing the ancient Asian teaching and the modern Western teaching together with one provocative and comprehensive phrase.[22] It is the "noble tension" I referred to in chapter 2, which is at the root of our human condition.

"Survival" in this sense, points to your ongoing anxiety about continuing to exist. No matter how secure and comfortable your life may seem, there is a raw, underlying question: Am I going to survive, or not? This question resides in your being just below the level of your conscious awareness. It is like an iceberg that has a hidden mass many times larger than the part you can actually see above the surface of the water.

THE EXPERIENCE OF PRIMORDIAL PANIC

You might wake up in the morning with a little head cold that you didn't have the night before. You might get a phone call telling you that some stranger has been using your credit card for the past few months. You might suddenly realize that you forgot all about a job interview you scheduled for that day. More dramatically, you might get an unexpected letter from your lover telling you that it's over or come home to an answering machine message that a dear friend your own age has had a massive stroke.

If you look closely at these experiences and are honest about what you find, your first sensation is undoubtedly panic. In the next moment, your human tendency is to quickly regroup and take whatever steps you can to correct or control the new situation. But if that isn't possible, you are left to feel the raw emotional reality of your relationship to your own vulnerability, or to the suffering of someone close to you. You are left with that same vulnerability you can never fully control or escape—the anxiety that is vibrating in you all the time.

Maybe this vibration is experienced on a low frequency, as background noise like the hum of your refrigerator or an automobile motor idling in the driveway next door. But when this background hum bursts right into the foreground of your life with experiences of sudden shock or loss of control, then the message of underlying panic about your survival is very direct and undiluted, and you can't cover it over anymore.

This experience is not the result of your neurosis. Instead it is built into the existential situation—the essence of which is that *you are trying to create something out of nothing all the time.*

TWO KINDS OF EGO

To understand this clearly, we need to distinguish between "ego" as Freud thought of it and "ego" as the Buddha and modern meditation masters such as my teacher use it. This is one of the most essential differences between Western and Buddhist ways of looking at the mind, and we will be returning to this difference again and again through the rest of the book.

In the most basic terms, Freud's ego is a psychological function. The word *ego* is Latin for "I," and represents a conscious, rational coping mechanism that enables us to live in the world with a certain measure of control and competence. From the point of view of survival, the ego is necessary and will always be necessary. Life in the world endlessly demands that you meet its challenges, and the ego does its best to rise to the occasion.

For the Buddha, ego is an existential distortion, an ongoing perceptual mistake. The Tibetan word for it literally means "grasping and fixating," which has an entirely different connotation than Freud's coping, managerial "I." "Grasping" and "fixating" refer to much deeper, less conscious tendencies of the mind to search compulsively for security and permanence, to fixate on things to reassure itself of the real existence of this security and permanence—and to ignore all evidence to the contrary.

It is this search that we are referring to when we talk about the desperate ongoing attempt to "create something out of nothing." According to the Buddha, this search can never finally succeed. *And this,* he teaches, *is the real source of our existential anxiety!*

When you closely examine your experience of nowness in meditation, you see with unmistakable clarity that you are struggling, moment after moment, to use your thoughts to pin down your constantly shifting experience. You are trying to give it an enduring reality that you can identify as "me" and "mine"—once and for all. But in trying to pin it down, you also see that you rob your nowness of its life. You are like a collector who captures beautiful butterflies in flight and then mounts them in a display case to preserve an experience of their beauty indefinitely. As William Blake wrote,

> He who binds to himself a joy
> Doth its winged life destroy;
> But he who kisses the joy as if flies,
> Lives in eternity's sunrise.[23]

The Buddha discovered that as long as he struggled to possess his nowness, he was caught in the tenacious grip of this anxiety. The only solution was to relax his struggle altogether.

TOUCH AND GO

From the Buddha's point of view, the existentialists only had it partially right. The sources of insecurity they describe—about death in the future, about aloneness and love, about meaning and the lack of meaning—are all ultimately bundled together into a much more immediate insecurity: that you are not quite real in any way that you can maintain securely in the face of constant change.

It is because of this unspoken fear that you experience the sense that your survival is at stake, even when it isn't. Even a situation that does not actually threaten your physical survival can initially provoke the same visceral reaction as one that does. Furthermore, maintaining your project of constantly making something out of nothing requires a tremendous amount of energy. This is part of the energy that moves through you when you practice meditation. It is your actual life force, but it is in the service of your efforts to constantly try to protect yourself.

SITTING IN THE FIRE

When you meditate, you stop trying to escape this anxiety, and you stop trying to protect yourself from this energy. Instead, as my teacher put it, you "use survival as a steppingstone." Rather than trying to ignore it or transcend it, you use the energy of this anxiety as a steppingstone to being more present and more fully awake. In this way, the practice of mindfulness incorporates and makes use of your survival instinct. To understand this fully is to understand accurately what we mean by "developing peace" in shamatha meditation.

Somewhere along the way in your path as a meditator, you stop trying to manufacture an experience of peace that will somehow shield you from the unpredictable energies of life. You are no longer *trying* to be peaceful. According to the Buddha, manufacturing peace in this way would create a kind of spiritual ego—a safe haven in which you can hide and make your spirituality into a cocoon. Doing this cuts you off from your life force; it's like trying to stop your heartbeat entirely so you don't have to experience it racing.

Instead, like a skillful rider on a wild horse, you stay right with the energy of your struggle and gradually tame it. To use another analogy, you do not try to put out the fire that you fear will consume you. You learn to sit right in the middle of it, because you realize that it was you who lit the fire in the first place. Therefore, only you can eventually bring the flames under control.

PRACTICING TOUCH AND GO IN NOWNESS

Engage fully with whatever comes up in your practice. Let your struggle itself be the object of mindfulness; you don't look elsewhere for your spirituality. The method for engaging the energy of your existential panic is called *touch and go*. This method addresses your instinct to survive very directly, as it meets your ego—that is, your habitual tendency to grasp and fixate on your experience—right at the moment it reappears.

When you practice touch and go, remember the first instruction for working with mental processes in shamatha: *don't suppress them as they arise, and don't chase them as they go.* What follows here is an expansion of this early instruction, down to the subtlest detail.

"Touch" challenges your instinct to evade the intensity of what is too threatening. When you "touch" an experience, you actualize your willingness to stay in contact with its rawness in the present moment of meditation, no matter what it is. When thoughts and especially emotions come up in practice, it is their energy you experience first. You actually experience it in the body before you have a clear consciousness of their content. By not suppressing this experience, you allow it to touch you. You stay with it, and accommodate it.

"Go" challenges your habit of holding onto your stories about what is happening in order to reassure yourself that you're still there. There is a crucial distinction here between the *energy* of your experiences and the *storylines* you create about them. This distinction is a vital instruction for all levels of Buddhist meditation.

The experience of energy happens before you can articulate or conceptualize the meaning of what is happening. You communicate this meaning to yourself as a narrative, or storyline. One of the main discoveries you make in fully engaging the practice of shamatha is that you spend most of your waking life telling yourself stories. Not only that but these stories have a repetitive quality, which reinforces their power to create emotional fixation.

When you "go," you don't cling to or cherish the storyline of any experience; rather after you have fully made contact by touching, you disown the experience and let it go. Because as thoughts and emotions become more fully developed, it is not their energy but their storyline that hooks you and makes you lose your mindfulness and give in to distraction. It's as if you are watching a movie and you forget it's only a movie, and then become so absorbed in the story that you even forget you're sitting in a theatre. By letting go of the storyline being played out on the screen of your mind, you come back to yourself again.

FAMILIARITY BREEDS THE COCOON

Your ego is equally adept at fixating on pleasurable *and* painful experiences alike. This is how the cocoon we discussed earlier is constructed. The reason for this is that, from the perspective of the cocoon, it is *familiarity*, not pleasure or pain in themselves, that is most vital to keeping it alive. Painful narratives have as much power to create fixation as pleasurable ones—if not more. Be it ever so painful, there's still no place like home.

My teacher once said that we spend our lives making mountains out of molehills and that meditation turns those mountains back into molehills again. The practice of touch and go dismantles the cocoon, one thread at a time. In the process, we learn that the stories we tell ourselves are not solid and real as we believed them to be, but begin as mere sensations, thoughts, and emotions that arise and pass away in nowness in shifty and dreamlike ways. Moment after moment, with gentleness and precision, we cut through our fixation on these stories, like popping soap bubbles with a feather.

Then we might even make the startling discovery that our pain is not a threat and our pleasure is not a promise. Each appears nakedly by itself in nowness, without an echo of past or future, hope or fear—and then passes away.

Inviting the Breeze of Delight

One of the double binds of your experience of the cocoon is the back-and-forth play between your longing to meditate and your resistance to doing it. The role of effort in mindfulness practice is another double bind because the practice of meditation requires effort on your part and does not simply happen to you. But, on the other hand, you must have the right understanding of effort or your practice will miss the mark in very fundamental ways.

If practice does not simply happen to you, do you make it happen? If so, how do you go about making it happen? These are important questions. We could talk about this effort on two levels. First, we could understand it as a technique in meditation. Then, and beyond that, we could appreciate it as an overall attitude—not only toward meditation but toward your life as a whole.

THE DECISIVE MOMENT

The technique of right effort in shamatha practice is to return from your involvement with thoughts and fantasies back to mindfulness of the body, of breathing, and of the simple reality of the present moment. This moment of returning happens over and over again. It is the decisive moment in practice, in which you actualize your intention to tame the wandering mind, here and now. You return because you recognize that there is no other place and no other time available to you other than now. It is a moment of truth, like the saying, "If not now, when? If not here, where? If not me, who?"

The key to cultivating right effort here is connected with *how* you bring the wandering attention back to the present moment. To take advantage of the mind's natural instinct to bring itself back from distraction, how you do it is with a sense of innocence and simplicity. You go along with the flow of that instinct. You allow it to happen to you. As my teacher instructed, the actual experience of this in your practice is that there is a sudden shift in the tone. Without any warning, you are back. You don't need to prepare yourself to come back or give yourself a pep talk or even a mandate. You don't need to argue with yourself about how one side thinks it would be a good idea to come back, but the other whines like a naughty child asking permission from an authority figure, "Couldn't I just hang out with this fantasy a little longer?" At that point, you are already back. So there is no warm-up, no prelude, for coming back.

Once you are back, you continue the effort's innocence and simplicity by resisting the urge to nurse the experience. You don't use it as an occasion to make a little monument to yourself. You don't congratulate yourself for having returned because you have an underlying assumption that coming back more frequently reflects how good you are at meditation. There is no patting your own back, no postgame celebration.

All of this—both preceding and following your return—is the internal dialogue of your ego, the incessant talking to yourself that keeps the illusion of the reality and permanence of that ego alive. My teacher called this process of overcomplication "entertaining the messenger." When a messenger arrives to give you a message, you read it, but it is unnecessary and inappropriate to invite him in for dinner as well. In the same way, instead of entertaining the messenger and being regaled with stories of the journey, you relate to the content of the message. In this case, the message is telling you to rest in mindfulness and awareness.

As you observe yourself returning to the present moment, the breath, and the posture, you may begin to wonder *who* is having this sudden experience of coming back? This is an excellent question, one that could eventually bring you to the deeper truth of what the Buddha called *egolessness.*

But for now, to the extent that we give it a label of any kind, we can call this observing consciousness the *naked witness.* My teacher called it the *abstract watcher.* These labels point to a simple, unselfconscious flash of the mind that is aware, on the most basic level, of coming back to itself. You are just back, once again, and this naked witness is just the flash of being back. This simplicity is the very heart of the mindfulness of effort.

DEFLATING THE DRAMA

From here, you continue to practice patiently with posture, breath, and thoughts just as you were instructed. Sometimes, especially when you have been caught up in a particularly juicy and compelling fantasy, it is helpful in the moment you recognize your distraction, to label it *Thinking* silently to yourself. This helpfully deflates the drama of your involvement with the fantasy. But notice that the label is an afterthought whereas the moment of recognition that you were distracted happens before you think at all. This is a profound point, and we will return to its implications later.

RIGHT EFFORT AND WRONG EFFORT

Effort can also be an overall attitude that creates the environment in which your practice—and indeed your whole life—happens. If there is a sense of allowing the flash of mindfulness to happen without manipulating it too much, the emphasis on effort as an overall attitude becomes more proactive.

It is unavoidable: you will bring to your relationship with meditation the same kinds of attitudes you bring to all the other activities you're involved in. If you tend to be ambitious and set on accomplishing great things, you will bring this ambition to meditation. If you tend to be solemn and pious, regarding your pursuits as deserving great weight and import, you will bring this dutifulness to meditation. But neither of these attitudes will provide you with the inspiration to fuel your effort over the long haul, so to speak. Each of them eventually collapses from its own weight.

OVERCOMING LAZINESS

After a discussion about effort, it might be useful to say a few things about *laziness*. Traditionally, laziness is regarded as the most serious obstacle to your ability to progress in meditation practice. If you can't get to the cushion in the first place, you have no starting point for the path. You have no way even to work with the other obstacles that will challenge you once you're sitting.

These other obstacles, which we will explore later, present themselves precisely because you've actually begun working with your habitual patterns, or what the Buddha called your *karmic obscurations*. You've actually begun to make a direct relationship with them at last because you're really doing the practice. The fact that such obstacles are coming up is good news—fantastically good news from the point of view of learning how to be a warrior. At last, you have met the "enemy," can see its face, begin gently to engage it, and become stronger, softer, and more fearless in the process. You are not lazy on the most basic level because you are engaging the work.

Laziness is the most dangerous obstacle because it stands right at the gate into the field of engagement and blocks it. If you don't enter, you have no opportunity even to experience the field where all the warriorship training actually takes place. There's a saying that "fifty percent of life is just showing up." Here we might say, "Fifty percent of practice is just getting to the cushion." The gift of returning spontaneously to the present moment again and again—the fruit of mindful effort—is granted only when you have first set the stage for it by regularly and patiently showing up for practice.

THREE KINDS OF LAZINESS

There are three kinds of laziness in relation to meditation practice. The first is *lethargy,* or procrastination. You don't want to make the effort or deal with any of the challenge or inconvenience such an effort might entail—even when you know it's a good thing to do. Even when you know the benefits, like cultivating a sane and joyful approach to your life rather than staying within your dark cocoon, you continually find reasons why now is not a good time to practice. You find endless excuses not to go to the cushion. Sometimes you convince yourself the excuse is valid. Sometimes you see right through it, and the queasiness of confronting that self-deception is enough to push you to the cushion. But more often, it is not enough.

The second kind of laziness is *having too many activities,* a neurotic approach of cocooning in workaholic tendencies. It's a high-energy style, where the wrong kind of effort— the roadrunner style of having so much to do and so many places to go all the time—has become a deliberate strategy of avoidance. It has become a way of not taking the time to face your state of being directly. As long as you can keep moving, you will not have to feel the immense underlying anxiety that is fueling your whole enterprise.

The third is *being disheartened* and is the result of habitual reliance on the first two kinds of laziness. You have lost hope, or faith, in yourself. It's a kind of depression, in which you fixate on the belief that you are an unworthy or unworkable person who cannot accomplish the practice, who is not capable of rising to the challenge of facing your mind. At the root of this is a loss of any sense of joy or delight in your existence. More than all the others, this form of laziness is deeply embedded in the suffocating heaviness of the cocoon, an almost physical sense of being weighed down by your experience of yourself.

The strategies of avoidance that laziness provides are woven into your cocoon, at the deepest level. Laziness is a powerful obstacle, and the many forms it takes in your daily life may not immediately be obvious.

What antidote can you apply to this formidable obstacle to spiritual development? The antidote lies in applying right effort—not just as a meditation technique—but as an overall attitude toward your life in general.

THE BREEZE OF DELIGHT

According to masters of meditation, you need to *fall in love* with wakefulness. Wakefulness has the qualities of simplicity and innocence, and even—sooner or later—it takes on a quality of joy. At a certain point, your longing for wakefulness becomes more powerful than your resistance, and you don't go back. The essence of this love is your tremendous appreciation for the unique value you receive through the discipline of becoming a warrior. Only love of this kind provides the energy necessary to sustain your ongoing exertion. Only love of this kind can eventually bring you to a state in which your life is unimaginable to you without this discipline.

Do not confuse this love with the idea that your practice should always be pleasurable or rewarding, or that you should always enjoy it because you are getting so much out of it. That would just be another form of self-deception. For it is not the experiences you have when you practice, but the wakefulness itself that you fall in love with.

The Shambhala teachings describe this joy, and the sense of appreciation it brings, as *the breeze of delight*. It is the felt experience of sudden wakefulness and the vividness of the way it contrasts with the feeling of being locked in your cocoon. It is as if you had opened all the doors and windows of a room that had been sealed for years with no ventilation and let fresh air enter for the first time in a long time.

Wakefulness is an experience of unconditional goodness. More and more, as you practice meditation, you begin to recognize this experience and to appreciate its incomparable value. Accessing it may be as simple as seeing a golden patch of sunlight on the wall of your bedroom when you wake up in the morning.

So the attitude of right effort in meditation and in life ultimately depends upon appreciation and joy. This cannot be manufactured, but it can be cultivated. You need only to make yourself available—again and again—so that the breeze of delight can come to you. All you have to do is return to the present moment and thereby open the window of your mind. When you do so, the disarming directness and power of meditation begins to become more apparent to you—and your longing for it grows and grows.

MINDFULNESS AND AWARENESS

The mind you experience in meditation is simply an unfolding of awareness, or knowingness. At the level of shamatha practice, what your mind knows is still experienced as if it were separate from you, *out there,* so to speak. One way of defining *mind* is to say that it is "that which has the capacity to be aware of something other than itself." You are the witness, and you're witnessing the contents of your mind. Recall the metaphor of the observer who sits comfortably on the bank of a stream, watching its flow. At this point, it is probably more helpful to think of *mind* as a verb rather than as a noun so that you don't forget you are dealing with a dynamic process rather than a concrete entity. What all forms of mindfulness meditation have in common is the simple truth that this dynamic knowingness is always there, *minding* things.

THE ONE-SHOT DEAL OF NOWNESS

The more deeply you are able to stabilize the mindfulness of shamatha, the more you realize the truth of what my teacher called "the one-shot deal of nowness." What he meant is that this mind you experience when you meditate—with all its busyness and speed, its highlights and emotional varieties, its melodramas, its ups and downs, its complicated schemes and strategies of all kinds—is really an ongoing process of great simplicity. This simplicity consists of the fact that this mind can only relate to the moment of nowness, and it can only do this one moment at a time.

Not only that, but the relationship between nowness and the object of your attention is choiceless. Whatever your mind is minding, that is its nowness. You may be having an elaborate fantasy about a past experience, but that fantasy *is* your nowness at that moment. There is no other present moment or nowness behind or apart from the fantasy, so to speak. And though you seem to be dwelling in the past, it is merely a memory that can only take place in nowness. From that point of view, there is no past—only memory in nowness.

Because your mind is generally moving so fast, and with such fickleness, most of the time you do not see this simplicity. We could describe this as a "neurotic mind," which keeps obscuring itself by means of its own chaotic movement. Or we could call it the "grasshopper mind" because it jumps impulsively back and forth with no apparent logic or reason. The practice of shamatha gradually tames this grasshopper mind. It slows it down, but not so that it becomes duller or less intelligent. Assuming that will happen is to mistake mental speed for cognitive sharpness. By slowing your mind down, it simply becomes clearer, more precise, and more able to see its own movement in the present moment. It does not overlook itself.

In the film from the late 1980s, *Buckaroo Banzai,* the hero gives a speech to his warrior comrades that ends with the punch line, "Remember, men, wherever you go, there you are." The mindfulness of the mind experienced in shamatha, then, is that same choiceless simplicity: either you are here, or you aren't. There is no escape from this one-shot deal of perception, moment after moment after moment. Mindfulness training is nothing more, and nothing less, than learning how to show up for the moment in this way.

This way of practicing meditation, which was also described in chapter 9, is *not too tight, not too loose. Not too loose* means that there must be precision when you meditate. You don't simply hang out idly and hope for the best. Instead, you appreciate the accuracy and simplicity of this one-shot deal. But *not too tight* means that if you make a big project out of being accurate and precise, you miss the moment because you are somehow adding something extra to the simplicity.

REFINING THE OBJECT OF MINDFULNESS

In terms of the technique of shamatha practice, you begin to *let part of your attention go to the breath and the rest to the general environment.*

To do this properly, begin to refine the way you use your breath as the object of mindfulness. That is, instead of resting your attention on the full movement of the breath in and out of the body, you focus now only on the breath as it goes out into the space around you. Raise your eyes and look out into the space, though with the same soft, relaxed gaze as in the initial instruction. If it is helpful to quantify, apply roughly 25 percent of your attention on the breath, 75 percent on the environment.

This changes your relationship to the technique of shamatha in a subtle but powerful way. Just as earlier you were practicing touch and go with thoughts, so now you begin to practice touch and go with the breath itself, as well. You tune into the moment of precision as the breath goes out, then you naturally let it dissolve into the openness. The breath dissolves as it goes out, and you don't sustain your attention to it as it comes back in. You begin to let go of the *project* of meditating.

With this style, there may be a more general sense that you are here, just sitting, aware of your posture, aware of the thoughts and sensations as they come up and pass away, aware of the physical situation around you where you're sitting, and so on. The precise quality of your mind being mindful is happening in a bigger space, so to speak. There is a sense of openness around the technique of relating to the breath. You don't have to nurse that experience of being mindful, like a clerk carefully checking and ringing up every item that goes past him at the checkout counter. While mindfulness remains a deliberate process, it does not become an obsessive one.

When you meditate like this, there is no longer any deliberate attention to the inbreath. Instead, only the outbreath is experienced in a definite, tangible way as the object of mindfulness. But each time the outbreath dissolves into space, you find that your mind may relax into a more open dimension. The invitation to relax within this open environment is implicit; you have already set the stage for it by placing one-pointed attention on the movement of your breath in the original instruction for shamatha.

THE EXPANSION INTO AWARENESS

As you come to rest in awareness, you might discover that this mind you are being mindful of is actually *full of gaps,* full of openness, as part of its natural pattern. You can't heavy-handedly pin down the present moment. That would be like a clumsy dancer who tries so hard to follow the music perfectly that he keeps stepping on his partner's toes. Instead, if you look closely, you begin to suspect that within this openness there is nobody in particular who is keeping this project of mindfulness going. It is more self-existing and simply happening on its own without too much help from you.

Now meditation becomes a balance of precision and freedom, of sharpness and openness. More and more, it becomes a kind of dance. There is the precise experience of the one-shot deal of nowness, and there are the "gaps" that lead to an open background of presence out of which the experience of the one-shot deal suddenly emerges, flashes, and passes away.

It is that simple—always!

There is much more going on than just the return to the breath, and you could tune into this bigger picture, more and more. Doing this is not so much a *technique* as a *discovery* that occurs naturally as you continue with the practice. In a more formal sense, this expansion in the practice is a gradual transition from *mindfulness* to *awareness.* These two words are being used here in very precise ways that are not interchangeable.

Mindfulness is the precision and the appreciation of detail that develops from working diligently with the shamatha technique of returning again and again to the object of attention. The focus and one-pointedness that develop from mindfulness are the indispensable foundation for all the meditative practices that come afterward.

Awareness is the experience of relating to the larger environment in which all these details are taking place. It is an appreciation of the *space* in which the details arise.

The Tibetan word for this awareness is *sheshin,* which means "presently knowing." It is a kind of panoramic alertness or intelligence that is always happening alongside the mindfulness as we continue to practice.

The Buddhist teachings offer two metaphors for how mindfulness and awareness relate: the army metaphor and the township metaphor.

Army Metaphor

If mindfulness is the general of an army, sheshin is the spy who does reconnaissance before the engagement on the battlefield happens. What this means in your meditation practice is that mindfulness—the general—leads the practice of shamatha by directing you to hold the posture, follow the instructions, feel sensations, and notice qualities of thought or breath. Sheshin—the spy—is the continual wake-up quality that brings you back to the object of meditation and alerts you to potential obstacles before they become too overwhelming. This advance intelligence works because it is familiar with the enemies (habitual patterns and distractions) and their troop strength (the power of the emotional hook). Sheshin is therefore sometimes referred to as a "light-handed warning system."

For example, if your mind is habitually wild and overly excited when you practice or habitually drowsy and dull, it is sheshin that becomes aware of the approach of these obstacles before they happen so that the general of mindfulness can deal with them by focusing on the posture, sensation, or the breath—and thereby keep you in the present moment. As you become more familiar with your habitual mental tendencies, the spy becomes sharper, and the feedback more useful in working with the obstacles to your practice.

Township Metaphor

In the second analogy, mindfulness is the town, sheshin is the sheriff, and the obstacles are the outlaws. Here, sheshin protects the town by rounding up the obstacles, before they take over.

One of the many ways to do this is to apply your awareness of the environment and arrange it deliberately for a desired effect, or outcome. A good example of this is contained in traditional Tibetan instructions for people engaged in solitary retreat. If your habitual mental mode is wildness, it is recommended that in order to subdue the mind you should wear heavier clothing, eat heavier food, create a warmer environment in your retreat space, move around less, and face a dark or black surface while meditating with a downward gaze. If your greatest obstacle is drowsiness, the opposite instructions are given: in order to perk up the mind, wear lighter clothing and eat lighter food, open the windows and allow more air circulation, intersperse your sessions of sitting meditation with frequent sessions of walking meditation, and face a bright or white surface as you sit with an upward gaze.

A DEEPER LEVEL OF KNOWING

The key aspect of sheshin is that it is a sustained experience of being present for whatever arises in the mind as you practice. In other words, whether your mind is still or full of thoughts, you are present with that, and you are right there for that. You are not constantly distracted, so you are not constantly coming back from that state of distraction. More and more, there is a continuity of wakefulness and presence. Most important, there is a noticeable deepening of the *knowing* faculty in your spiritual development.

Another way to say this is that there is a subtle, continuous experience of the *abstract watcher* or *naked witness* in your meditation practice. This experience includes a sense that whatever your mind is doing, the qualities of presence and alertness are there. They don't change from moment to moment, and they aren't undermined by temporary occurrences in the mind.

The alert awareness, or sheshin, becomes panoramic—wider and more encompassing than that little dot of mindfulness, the "little dot" being the vividness of each detail of mindful perception as it flashes into existence in the present moment. Sheshin tunes us into the background—the larger environment of *presence* that is always there. The "background" is the open, unconditional dimension of that vivid experience—an openness that both precedes the dot and remains after it has vanished.

To summarize, mindfulness is the dot of nowness, and presence is the abiding space of awareness in which the moment of mindfulness vividly flashes then passes away, over and over again.

OBSTACLES TO PRACTICING
PEACEFUL ABIDING

When you really try to make a connection with the practice of shamatha, obstacles generally do arise. In this chapter and the one that follows, you will find a traditional approach to understanding and overcoming these obstacles that is like going to a doctor, receiving an accurate diagnosis of your ailment, and then taking the right medicine to relieve it. But in this case, you are learning to be both patient and doctor simultaneously.

Shamatha practice helps cultivate a mind that is less distracted. An undistracted mind is a tamed mind. A tamed mind is also less conflicted, less hard on itself, more kind to itself. It is a gentle mind. You cause less harm to yourself and therefore, less harm to others.

You cultivate an intention—and a state of being—which causes less harm and chaos in the world. In this way, the practice of meditation tames your state of mind and your conduct. When you bring your strong intention to accomplish these things to your practice, things tend to open up.

Shamatha practice is not a way of creating these things in yourself, but of working through the obstacles to experiencing them that you have built up over time. As the Buddha emphasized again and again, these positive qualities are innate to the mind, and they can be dug out and cultivated like plants in a dormant garden. Through meditation, you dig into the earth of your mind, and when you commit yourself to the practice, you begin to see recurrent patterns of thought, emotion, and action that get in the way of these qualities. These patterns are the obstacles that prevent you from being fully present with yourself.

THE LIGHT OF AWARENESS

The traditional analogy is that the sun is the basic nature of our mind, and these patterns are clouds that cover it. The sun is always there, but the clouds block our experience of its full brilliance. Because these clouds often cast a cold and dark shadow, you may mistake them for signs that you are fundamentally bad or condemned. But, in fact, they are simply the result of habitual patterns of thought, emotion, and action that have been with you a long time. They are patterns of avoidance. The good news is that, like clouds, these patterns are fleeting and temporary blockages. Even in Seattle, cloud cover is not permanent.

Meditation practice exposes these obstacles to the light of your awareness and makes them more obvious. This is why sometimes when you practice—especially at the beginning—it feels like things are getting worse. Really they are just becoming more obvious; it has become impossible to pretend they don't exist, and they are that much harder to ignore.

These obstacles are the defense mechanisms of ego. They are a bit like the inky substance that a squid squirts out into the water behind it to keep predators from seeing it and catching it. So these obstacles are the ink, ego is the squid, and your wakefulness is the predator. This analogy recalls the environment of the cocoon. Ego has gone into hiding and uses the obstacles as camouflage because wakefulness threatens its dull, repetitive, yet familiar, world.

BRINGING KINDNESS TO THE SIX OBSTACLES

There are six obstacles in shamatha practice. Before describing them, it's important to emphasize that there's no need for any sense of judgment or condemnation about the fact that you experience them. In fact there could be a lot of humor in seeing how familiar they are. All of us, without exception, experience these obstacles at some time or another. No one need pretend to be perfect; everyone has his or her own stuff to work with.

Being able to name and identify the obstacles is actually a very cheerful process, like identifying strange insects that suddenly land on you in a jungle. You look at them up close and notice how strange they are with their little legs and their many colors.

Laziness

The first obstacle is *laziness,* which I discussed in chapter 15 in relation to the mindfulness of effort. Here, laziness has a very precise meaning. It's a resistance to the entire practice of meditation altogether. Much of the challenge in meditation practice is found in just getting yourself to the cushion. Laziness is experienced as a kind of heaviness that comes up when you even think about practicing or in the moments when you are about to go to the cushion. It's as if your feet suddenly have lead weights on them and you can't get there. This resistance makes it so difficult just to start because it's a state of mind that looks for a way out of just going and doing it. The subconscious verbalization that goes with it is something like *I just don't feel like practicing today. Maybe tomorrow.*

Forgetfulness

The second obstacle is *forgetfulness.* Forgetfulness happens despite the fact that you have been instructed in the technique and the purpose of it. You can often sit for a very long time without using the technique in which you were instructed at all. As a result, your practice is like an ongoing fog of discursive thought. You forget to come back to the breath, and you have no ability to cut through your involvement with thinking to rest in nowness. Sometimes you might meditate and afterward look back and realize you didn't come back to the breath once. Your allegiance is to forgetfulness instead of to wakefulness.

Drowsiness

The third obstacle is *drowsiness accompanied by depression.* This drowsiness/depression is an actual physiological experience of fatigue, but the tiredness arises out of psychological fixation. This fixation is the tendency of your mind to dwell in the lower realm of experience, which consists of feelings of extreme poverty and grasping or intense aggression or a stupefied state in which you don't care.

When your mind is simmering in this thick stew of negative emotions, the body follows, and the direct connection between mind and body becomes obvious. Your posture slumps, your head bobs, your gaze films over, your hands slip off your thighs. It's as if while you were wading through the swamp of your own mind, your body just became exhausted with the effort.

Of course you may experience drowsiness when you have not gotten enough sleep. But I'm not talking about that level. This level is the fatigue brought about by dwelling in unwholesome mental states for long periods of time without being aware of it.

Wildness

The fourth obstacle is *wildness,* which is energetically the opposite of heavy qualities of drowsiness; it's an extreme lightness, as if gravity released its hold on you and you are no longer anchored to the earth. In this experience, your mind jumps all over the place like a grasshopper. There is wildness and even craziness. Your little thoughts gather and increase in volume until they crescendo into huge cosmic schemes. Small molehills become huge, fantastical mountains, and you tend to ride that energy as long and far as you can to avoid simply being present. In the first fifteen minutes of sitting, you could build up to being master of the universe, then crash in the last fifteen minutes. It's like the stock market on an extreme cycle of ups and downs. These grandiose fantasies of hope and fear dissipate your energy. There is tremendous mental speed.

It is also said that this obstacle arises when you have second thoughts about your connection with practice altogether or even an extreme regret that you ever got involved with it in the first place. It's as if meditation becomes a prison that constricts your wildest ambitions and your fondest dreams. Sitting becomes a downer and an insult to your amazing cosmic possibilities.

Carelessness

The fifth obstacle is *carelessness*. This obstacle can be summarized by the phrase, "Why bother?" You understand the practice, you understand the meaning behind it, and you understand that it's a good thing to do and why. You know that you should tame your mind, but somehow you just can't be bothered. To some degree this resembles laziness, but its underlying motivation is more defensive; you don't really believe in yourself. You feel you can't do it, that you are not worthy of doing it, so carelessness is your last line of defense so that you don't have to do it. You just can't be bothered; it's just too hard.

Being careless, overly casual, or having an attitude of dismissiveness—all these variations are covers for feeling unworthy and incapable of accomplishing meditation practice. So you make light of it and express disrespect for it, but truly, you feel disrespect for yourself. *Maybe other people can do this, but I can't. Everyone else is a potential Buddha except me, so who cares?* That twist of defensiveness is at the core of this obstacle.

Unable to Coordinate the Whole Thing

The sixth and last obstacle is called *not being able to coordinate the whole thing*. The basic idea here is that your intention is good, but your resolve is weak. Caught in the trap of good intentions, you are easily distracted from your commitment, and the whole thing is somehow a little bit too soft and a little too mushy. There's the feeling that you could really do this and that you'll get around to it eventually, but your schedule is insanely full; it's very hard to find the time to fit practice in anywhere. So you lose focus and purpose. You lose your one-pointed attention. Your relationship to meditation takes on a hit-and-miss quality. You realize that you really have to do it and that just having the intention to do it is not quite enough. But you can keep yourself company with your good intentions constantly, yet not really be practicing.

It's even more important to have the right attitude toward these obstacles than to identify them. If you name them purely as a catalog by which you can then punish yourself, it would be very unfortunate. If you can take a light attitude toward the obstacles, full of simple curiosity, the more confidence you will have that they are not permanent or immoveable. Rather, it is clear that they are temporary obscurations covering over your fundamental strength and wakefulness within.

Regard them as accurate and useful little messages about what happens to you and to everyone else who commits to this noble discipline. Have faith that they are temporary, that they can be worked with, and that they can be transformed into wakefulness.

Overcoming the
Obstacles to Peace

We overcome the obstacles in shamatha by applying remedies or antidotes. Two themes run through all of them:

- Take a cheerful attitude toward yourself.
- Develop greater synchronization between your mind and body, your intention and execution.

Cheerfulness and synchronization of body and mind are like two currents of energy and commitment that run through all the antidotes in shamatha meditation and propel realization. More skill and greater strength in applying the antidotes come with time and experience.

ANTIDOTES TO LAZINESS

Of the eight antidotes, four are applied to *laziness*. This is a clear message that laziness is the most powerful and therefore, the hardest of the obstacles to overcome. It's the ground or starting point—or nonstarting point actually, because if you can't even get yourself to the cushion, you have no opportunity to work with the other obstacles at all.

The four antidotes to laziness have a progression, and each has an organic logic within that progression. As you study them, you might reflect on this.

Faith

The first antidote is *faith*. This particular kind of faith has nothing to do with religious faith but instead has to do with cultivating trust in the practice itself. Because you have had glimpses of the beneficial effects of the practice and its qualities of strength and goodness, you feel that meditating is the right thing to do. Even in the midst of your laziness and resistance, there is some part of you that knows practicing is a good thing to do, a helpful thing to do. You feel that it's healthy to be involved with the Dharma, that it's not crazy to be involved with at all. You feel that it is fundamentally healthy to engage in practice and to study the teachings because it strikes you as straightforward and sane. You have faith that this is the case. While it may not be a faith you can articulate, it is a powerful intuitive confidence in the path.

The pioneering teacher Alan Watts made a compelling distinction between belief and faith. He said that belief is the wish that the truth turn out to be what you want it to be, whereas faith is a basic openness to the truth whatever it may turn out to be. He said, "Faith has no preconceptions; it is a plunge into the unknown. Belief clings, but faith lets go."[24]

This openness is the essence of the nontheistic practices the Buddha taught. Your faith is not placed in the expectation that someone else will save you. Instead, you are working with your own mind and resources and developing your own positive qualities, and faith in your own capacity for awakening is an essential part of this. It can take you a long way—all the way in fact!

Respect

The second antidote to laziness is *respect.* It is also referred to as "having a sense of sacredness." This sacredness goes beyond the conventional religious understanding—the idea that because God gave an ancient decree that something is sacred, therefore, it must be so. This kind of decree has left humanity with many empty rituals that hang on long after people have ceased to believe in them.

This kind of sacredness is very up-to-date and in the moment. It's the sense that your life is worth respecting, that it is worth taking good care of. Your environment is worthy of tending to. You are also worth treating well, and you can do so without self-indulgence, making demands, or engaging in wretched excess of any kind. Sacredness here means that your life has an inherent dignity. You respond by wanting to cultivate the presence of that natural dignity in your life because you respect it and yourself, both. This respect is why you don't trash yourself or your environment at all. It's an attitude that makes you want to clean up your home and put fresh flowers on the table. You feel that your life is worth cleaning up and adorning.

Respect is an important antidote to laziness because what happens with laziness, both in your practice and in your life, is that your world begins to fall apart around the edges. It begins to fray at the collar or the cuffs because you stop taking care of things properly. In this way, respect is bringing the attitude of sacredness to all the ordinary details of your life. Meditation is one of those ordinary details; you attend to it daily as a vital part of your well-being, just as weekly you attend to taking out the garbage and organizing the recyclables.

Effort

The third antidote to laziness is *effort.* Here you actively work with the inspirations that come from having faith and respect. Faith and respect are powerful positive mindsets, but effort is the expression of the adage that actions always speak louder than words. Effort is the way you embody the faith and respect, the way you actualize them by applying them in activity. You know deep inside that after all the talking about it and thinking about it, you have to do it. You know that your good intention is not quite enough and that in order to actually make it real, effort is required. In chapter 15, I described the right way to relate to effort—as an expression of appreciation and even joy—and it may be helpful to reread from within this new application of effort as an antidote to laziness.

As my teacher used to say, "Just do it." Nike must have stolen the line from him! Because it's a good one.

Completely Processed

The fourth and last antidote to laziness is called *shinjang*. This is a Tibetan word that means "completely processed." My teacher used to compare it to a cotton shirt that's been worn many times and washed many times. As a result, it fits you really well. It's very soft and pliable and comfortable, and you always look forward to wearing it.

Similarly, when faith and respect are mixed again and again with effort, the experience of shinjang arises. This is how you feel after you've practiced diligently and regularly for a long time. Your body and mind *do* become more synchronized. There is a greater sense of relaxation, and your mind has become flexible. There is a growing feeling that going to the meditation cushion, sitting down on it, and practicing is not something that is being imposed on you. Rather, it feels like the natural expression of your dignity as a human being. To sit upright in good posture, to work with your mind in a disciplined, gentle way—that is how to be a human being, in the best sense. The more you practice with shinjang, the more you relax into the dignity of who you really are.

From this point of view, practice is not a punishment. Neither is it a form of self-improvement nor a form of self-correction. You are flipping that attitude around altogether by understanding that practice is how you truly and fully express yourself as a human being. Perhaps no dharma teacher has been more eloquent in bringing this point home than Shunryu Suzuki Roshi, the Japanese Zen master who, beginning in 1959, pioneered the teaching of buddhadharma in the West. Throughout his book *Zen Mind, Beginner's Mind* Suzuki Roshi seems to be talking about this very subject. Practice, he says, is "just resuming our basic nature." He loves to use the word "resume"—as if we had gotten sidetracked for awhile, but then came back and sat in meditation and realized, "Oh yes, what a relief. I'm back. This is the best. This is it. This is my life. Whatever it is, this is what it is right now, and I'm right here with it, and it is good. There is no need to avoid or postpone because this is it."[25]

With shinjang comes a quality of cheerfulness that you actually experience in your body. Because as you give up your resistance to simply going and doing the practice, there is a sense of relaxation as you ease into it. You slide into meditation the way a seal slips into water—so symbiotic it's as if you were the same. That's shinjang. It's the fruition that arises from faith, respect, and continual effort—the willingness to just do it.

Antidote to Forgetfulness

The fifth antidote applies to the obstacle of forgetfulness, in which you forget the instructions for the technique or forget to apply what you have learned. This remedy is described as *having a folksy attitude* and is an extension of shinjang. It's taking the attitude that practice is an ordinary and natural thing to do. Practice is not something strange or foreign that has been imposed on you. You don't have to fight it because it isn't an alien. It's like taking a shower to get clean—you just remember what to do because it has become second nature.

When you make a big deal out of meditation practice, you set up a constant battle with it. You begin to feel that the technique has been forced on you and that the only way you can express your rebellion is to forget what was taught as often as possible. What starts as resistance to the technique sets the stage for forgetfulness.

I once saw a cartoon of a dog standing at a pharmacist's counter and the druggist is handing the dog a bottle of pills. The caption reads, "Here. Just find someone to force one of these down your throat every six hours." If you ever come to regard your meditation teacher as the pharmacist, the meditation practice as the pill, and your sense of discipline as the one force-feeding the medicine, you will soon find yourself up against the obstacle of forgetting.

Having a folksy attitude toward your practice cuts through the sense that practice is being forced on you. My teacher used to have little slogans that he gave students to remind them to take this attitude, such as "No big deal" and "Couldn't care less." They were reminders not to take the whole thing too seriously in the wrong way but instead suggestions to allow it to become a simple, ordinary expression of your life like brushing your teeth or eating breakfast.

Take the view that your practice is like a good friend you invite over to your home without thinking about it. It's such an ordinary gathering that you don't even have to get your calendars out to plan it.

ANTIDOTES TO DROWSINESS AND WILDNESS

The sixth antidote is for two obstacles: drowsiness and wildness. It is called the *light-handed warning system*. This is nothing other than the sheshin awareness described in the spy and sheriff analogies in chapter 16.

The basic point here is first, to recognize that the obstacle is approaching before it overwhelms you and second, to use the energy of the obstacle itself to wake you up, which you accomplish by not fighting with the obstacle while you're sitting on the cushion.

For example, when you experience drowsiness, the harder you struggle with it, the sleepier you become. Your panic about not falling into a pit of fatigue and keeling over on your cushion becomes a self-fulfilling prophecy. It invites the very outcome you're struggling so hard to avoid. You fall asleep and then jerk awake, over and over again. The deeper issue here is that we all have a conceptual ideal of the meditative experience that we aspire to have and regard any experience that doesn't measure up to it as a mistake or a failure. We would always like what we imagine to be a better nowness than the one we're having. As a result, we are caught in the hope and fear that arises in this gap between what we want and what we have. In this sense, what we experience in meditation is a mirror for the way we approach all of our life experiences off the cushion.

The only way to untie this knot is to relax with the experience you're having. Therefore, the meaning of *light-handed warning system* here is that when dullness and drowsiness approach, you recognize their presence as another opportunity to be gentle with yourself.

I recall one particular session of group meditation that took place during a month-long intensive. We had been sitting for many hours and several of us were fighting to stay awake. Our heads were bobbing like buoys on our shoulders. Then a very large man sitting directly across from me suddenly toppled over to the floor like a falling tree. The woman sitting next to him screamed, and everyone abruptly woke up and stayed wide-awake for the rest of the session.

Because you can't always rely on this kind of help from the external world, when you're dealing with drowsiness, the key is to not resist it. Go along with the feelings of drowsiness and tune into them as a way of staying present. Many people regard falling asleep on the cushion as a personal failure and so try to force themselves to stay awake. Instead, let yourself nod off and then wake up. It happens quickly, and you can watch the sensations, feelings, and even flashes of dreams come and go. In other words, simply transfer your mindfulness to the experience of falling asleep.

The antidote to wildness is the same in the sense that you do not struggle with its energy while it's happening out of your wish or your anxiety that you should be having a different kind of experience. The light-handed warning system here is connected with recognizing the approach of wildness through symptoms in your body and mind such as mental speed, agitation, vivid fantasy, and a general sense of being unmoored from the ground like a rising hot-air balloon.

Recall again the image of the spy in the awareness practice of sheshin. You become more sensitive to all the symptoms of the obstacle, then allow it to come along without forcibly trying to change its energy. This brings a deeper understanding of the meaning of *peaceful abiding* because the energy of wildness seems anything but peaceful. You let it play itself out rather than struggling to subdue it. In my own experience, putting slightly more emphasis on the feeling of the posture and on the felt experience of the full movement of the breath can also be helpful. It seems to be yet another way of finding the balance of "not too tight, not too loose."

In traditional Tibetan teachings on shamatha, there are very literal antidotes that are used for drowsiness and wildness, several of which were discussed in chapter 16. For example, if you're drowsy, you can face a bright white surface when you meditate because the brightness will naturally perk up your mind. If you don't have a white surface available, then you could visualize a white dot or sphere in front of you and slightly above the level of your head.

On the other hand, if your mind is wild, you can use black instead because it sobers the mind and brings it down and grounds it more. In the case of a black dot or sphere, you would visualize it closer to the level of the ground. So in both cases there is an appreciation that these are energetic states, and we are learning how to respect and become more sensitive to them. In other words, it can awaken your intelligence so that you become more curious and look more deeply at the habitual patterns that are fueling these extremes of energy that are so recurrently present in your mind and body.

ANTIDOTE TO CARELESSNESS

The seventh antidote is for carelessness, which is described as "intense awareness." Sometimes it's called "returning to mindfulness." Carelessness arises from an underlying sense that you are powerless over your own life experience. Because you feel powerless, you don't bother, which results in sloppiness. Through intense awareness, you take matters into your own hands. You resolve to work with it. Rather than feeling that your mind is stupid and unworkable, you take the attitude that you can shape it and that meditation is the means to do so. You can shape your mind toward natural discipline, toward wakefulness.

The idea here is to remember that your mind is workable and that you can shape your mind with confidence, as if you were a sculptor working with clay. You can actually do it. This attitude of workability empowers you. When you bring loving-kindness to this process, rather than using intense awareness as a further way to beat yourself up, you develop patience and gentleness.

The traditional analogy is to imagine yourself as your own child and to try to think how soft your approach is when you teach a child something new. A child needs that kind of attention in order to learn, so you don't give up, and you offer lots of encouragement along the way.

A careless attitude results from feeling powerless because your self-criticism tells you that you're an unworkable person. In response, you can become your own mother or father in the best sense. It is as if the kind, steady adult within you provides the uncertain child within you the patient support and encouragement it needs to begin standing on its own.

ANTIDOTE TO LACK OF COORDINATION

The eighth and last antidote is called *balance,* or *equilibrium.* This antidote is for the obstacle of not being able to coordinate the whole thing. This coordination is connected with the balance between attending to the little details of your life while at the same time having an overall sense of the environment in which they occur. If you're too focused on details, you lose the bigger picture, but if you're too enamored of the big picture, you tend to space out and ignore the details.

When my teacher described this antidote, he pointed out that this sense of balance applied both to shamatha practice and to your daily life. Essentially, he was talking about the proper balance between mindfulness and awareness. Once again, we are using the faculty of sheshin—the spy who gives the general of mindfulness useful intelligence about the troop strength of the "enemy"—with the enemy in this case being all the distractions that keep us from achieving the proper balance between our meditation practice and our other daily activities.

CHEER UP, LADIES AND GENTLEMEN

Generally speaking, the obstacles to shamatha practice are the result of being too hard on ourselves. Each antidote tells us to cheer up, realize we can synchronize our good intention with our discipline, and see that meditation is a very natural and ordinary thing to do.

When Chögyam Trungpa taught about Shambhala warriorship, he would sometimes open a golden fan to illustrate the brilliant quality of our awareness when it comes out from behind the clouds of these temporary obstacles. He called it the Great Eastern Sun because it is always ready to dawn in our experience if we simply turn and face in the right direction.

He would playfully exclaim, "Cheer up, ladies and gentlemen!" as he smiled broadly and opened the golden fan fully, holding it up for all of us to see. In that moment, it was impossible not to cheer up.

In these lines from the poem "Shoveling Snow with Buddha," Billy Collins playfully expresses the two themes of synchronizing your mind and body and taking a cheerful attitude toward your practice, as he imagines the Buddha helping him clear his driveway on a winter morning.

> He has thrown himself into shoveling snow
> as if it were the purpose of existence,
> as if the sign of a perfect life were a clear driveway
> you could back the car down easily
> and drive off into the vanities of the world
> with a broken heater fan and a song on the radio.[26]

PART THREE

THINGS AS THEY SEEM, THINGS AS THEY ARE

The Insights That Lead
to Enlightenment

Vipasyana is a Sanskrit word that means "clear seeing" or "direct insight." Vipasyana is the practice that led not only to the Buddha's attainment of enlightenment but also the enlightenment of all the great practitioners who have lived since then. Vipasyana is the purest expression of the "sudden" intelligence that enables the Buddhist spiritual path to happen at all.

WHAT PEACEFUL ABIDING
TRAINS YOU TO KNOW

Shamatha is the foundation for vipasyana in the sense that shamatha tames the wildness of your mind over time. When your mind is tamed, you can begin to see yourself clearly and simply for the first time. Shamatha is not actually concerned with the true nature of that seeing. It's only concerned with slowing the whole process down and stabilizing it.

The knowing developed through shamatha is still very much a dualistic knowing, in the sense that you are always checking back to evaluate the meditation. You are checking back to make sure that you are holding your mind to the object of attention—the breath. You are checking back on the energy of your mental state, asking, "Is the meditation wild today, or is it dull? Am I alert or am I sleepy? Are there a lot of thoughts and activity in my mind, or is it relatively still?" In this way, shamatha knows what the mind is doing moment-by-moment and whether you are present or not. It knows what the quality of your present experience is. It knows *sound of the car passing outside the window.* It knows *I'm thinking, how soon is lunch? because I'm getting hungry.* It knows *that patch of light on the floor has moved since I last noticed it.* We could say that shamatha is the *mere* knowing of things happening on the surface.

Of course this is a very important knowing because it is the difference between being present for your life or not!

In shamatha, we regard this knowing as an entity and refer to it as *one* who knows. We call it the *meditator* or the *witness* or the *abstract watcher.* All of these terms convey the understanding that shamatha is strengthening your ability to see the activity and movement of the mind without being caught up in it, overly identified with it, or swept away by it. In place of the scattered, anxious person you thought you were, now you feel yourself to be a more grounded, "together" person. This is the result of cultivating the witnessing mind through shamatha practice.

To further appreciate the profound importance of this for our quality of life, consider what psychologist William James observed more than one hundred years ago: "The faculty of voluntarily bringing back a wandering attention, over and over again, is the very root of judgment, character, and will." He added that training students to strengthen such a faculty should become the basis of their education and that such an education would be "an education *par excellence.*"[27]

AN EVEN DEEPER KNOWING

Vipasyana is the gateway into a deeper knowing than this. In fact, all the teachings that the Buddha gave about suffering, the nature of suffering, and how suffering can be healed or transcended are the result of the insight gained through his practice of vipasyana.

As you practice shamatha, vipasyana arises as the recognition that there is no underlying self who is having this experience of being present, simply aware, and undisturbed by the flow of thoughts and strong emotions. In other words, vipasyana is the recognition that this meditator in shamatha practice—this witness who has finally become so still and stable through patient, diligent practice—is just another thought. It's a very subtle and enjoyable thought, to be sure! But it is nothing more substantial than that. To put it another way, when you look deeply into the nature of the meditator who is practicing shamatha, you will not find anything that you can pinpoint as substantial or real. There is just knowingness; there is not *someone* who knows. In shamatha there is always someone who knows; in vipasyana there's just the knowing itself.

When vipasyana arises, the experience of meditation becomes extremely open and fluid because you are no longer checking back to a reference point of any kind. There is no "I" or "me" who is having this experience.

THE PATH OF TAMING THE SENSE OF "ME"

The "me" that you encounter when you first begin to practice shamatha is a wild, scrambled nexus of habitual patterns of struggle, neurotic speed, and hope and fear. Shamatha tames and soothes these recurrent patterns so that they have less painful influence or control over your moment-to-moment experience. If you stay with the practice, this gradual taming and slowing is a real, inevitable accomplishment. Traditionally, the mind of a practitioner is described in a series of metaphorical images of water.

At first, experiencing the mind is like standing under a waterfall. In the next stage, it is like sitting by a cool, swiftly flowing brook.

Next, it is like sitting by a slow, broadly flowing river. Finally, it is like sitting next to the ocean on a calm day.

This gradual process of slowing and taming creates a more subtle experience of "me." Rather than a confused me, it's a calm, clear me. In Western psychological language, we could say that the practice of shamatha leads to the experience of a healthy sense of self. But inevitably there's a fixation on that sense of health. As long as you're dwelling on that chilled-out version of yourself that shamatha has enabled you to experience and enjoy, you are blocking deeper knowing and intelligence. In other words, you could become addicted to shamatha and stop there. Of course, this would not be a terrible thing or even a bad thing! Beyond the sense of well-being it brings you personally, a tamed, gentle mind is a wonderful tool to wield. With it, you can refrain from contributing further to the pain and chaos that already exist all over the world.

But there is more to understand and realize personally, if you are so inspired.

HOW STILLNESS LEADS TO SEEING NONSELF

To use Western psychological terminology again, the healthy sense of self we experience in shamatha is a foundation, or gateway, for the experience of nonself in vipasyana. *Nonself* does not imply that you become a confused, dissociated fog of incoherent impressions or a self-absorbed victim incapable of functioning in the world. On the contrary, this experience of nonself—which is the essence of the Buddha's discovery of wakefulness—turns out to be the ultimate expression of clarity, aliveness, and responsiveness that a human being can realize. Here is an analogy for how shamatha leads to vipasyana:

> Imagine a lake whose surface has been stirred up by strong wind. The surface is never calm or still, but

constantly disturbed by waves and billows. Not only that, but sediment has been stirred up on the bottom as well, clouding the water and making it opaque, so that you can't see into it.

This is an analogy for your mind before you practice shamatha. The winds and sediment together represent strong habitual patterns of neurosis; the resulting cloudiness and turbulence of the water represents the felt experience of living under their painful influence all the time. To take the metaphor a step further, the winds are your present experience of painful emotional patterns, and the sediment is the accumulation of past imprints of all those experiences.

Now imagine that the strong winds subside. As a result, the surface of the water becomes still, the sediment settles again to the bottom, and the water becomes clear so that you can see into its depths, perhaps even all the way to the bottom.

This is an analogy for your mind after you have practiced both shamatha and vipasyana. The practice of shamatha causes the strong energies of neurosis to subside and the resulting agitation and confusion to lift as your mind becomes more clear and still. With these conditions, vipasyana can happen because nothing is obscuring your vision and you can see into the very depths of the lake.

This is a traditional analogy. A more contemporary, very simple analogy might be defrosting the windshield on a cold morning in order to see the road and drive to your destination. Shamatha is the defrosting process. Vipasyana is the clear view of the road that results, which enables you to drive safely.

NONSELF IN MEDITATION PRACTICE

During your meditation experience, here are a few simple things you can observe that show how vipasyana emerges from shamatha.

When Sense Perceptions Are Labeled

While practicing shamatha, look at your experience of a sense perception. For example, you hear a sound. Your mind immediately knows that this is a sound, and it will also immediately identify precisely what the sound is by labeling it: *that's a car going by the window.* Notice first how this labeling process occurs almost instantaneously after hearing the sound. You can observe the minute shift as you move very quickly from the pure nowness of the sound to identifying and labeling what it is, effectively making it part of your familiar conceptual world. That observation of your mind's activity offers a first glimpse of the direct knowing of vipasyana. It is recognizing that there is a difference between the immediate experience of your sense perception and the thought-label by which you tell yourself what you have just experienced. This ability to distinguish between direct experience and conceptual overlay is profoundly important at every stage of the path. My teacher called it the difference between *first thought* and second thought: first thought is your direct experience, and second thought is the interpretation you place on that experience.

When You Look for the Experiencer

But you can now take the investigation further. You can look to see if there is actually someone who is experiencing the sound. Can you find any actual dividing line between the experience of the sound and the one who is having that experience? Can you really separate the subject and the object?

No matter how often you investigate this perception, you cannot find a concrete dividing line of someone experiencing it and the experience itself. It is a single unitary moment of vivid knowing. The sound and the hearing of the sound are simultaneous. After the fact you say, *I heard the sound of the car passing.* But those are just conceptual labels. You think, *the sound of the car was out there, and I heard it.* But the thought process is a dim echo of the original perception. In fact, the thought process by its very nature demands a subject and an object, a noun and a predicate. These are the embedded conventions of your thought and your language.

There is not an underlying problem with this, as long as you see them for what they are—mutually agreed-upon conventions by which you make the world you experience intelligible to yourself and others when you communicate with each other. But the moment you begin to assume that these thought-conventions are the real essence of what you know about reality, you miss the pure wakefulness that underlies them and that, in a sense, precedes them.

If you like, you can now take the curiosity of vipasyana even further with this simple experience of hearing the sound of the car. You can ask yourself, *Is there really a distinction to be made between the first thought—the sound itself—and the second thought—the immediate identification of that sound as a car passing by on the street outside?* If you consider it from within your experience of linear time, you can say, *Yes, the experience came first and the thought followed right after, so in that sense they were different.* And you would be right, as far as the convention of linear time goes.

When You See Beyond "Inside" and "Outside"
But if you ask the same question from the point of view of the *essence* of each of those experiences, you will arrive at a very different conclusion. You will recognize that both the first thought

and the second thought are identical in the sense that they are moments of pure knowingness, pure awareness.

The first is traditionally called *appearance,* while the second is at the level of "thought." The first seems to be coming from outside you, that is, the sound; the second seems to be coming from inside you, that is, the thought about the sound. But in their very essence, they are the same flashes of pure awareness—nothing more and nothing less—and locating them "outside" or "inside" is, once again, just conceptual labeling.

When You See Beyond How Things Seem to How They Are

Look at the blue sky now. Notice your ingrained tendency to label what you look at, and try to simply look without labeling. If you catch yourself labeling it, see that the actual appearance of the blue sky does not depend on you telling yourself that it is blue. It doesn't depend on your label. That's going beyond concept to direct perception, and this direct perception is never based on "me." It is based simply on the awareness itself.

One of the most powerful moments in the film *The Girl with the Pearl Earring* occurs when Jan Vermeer is teaching his housekeeper to see the way an artist sees. They are looking out the window in his studio, and he asks her to tell him what color the sky is. She looks and immediately tells him, "It's blue." He tells her to look again more carefully. Gradually Vermeer brings her to see that what she assumed was blue is actually a whole palette of subtle colors—different shades of blue, grey, yellow, pink, and white. And of course they are constantly shifting and changing in nearly imperceptible ways.

Here we see the real power, the real point and importance of vipasyana. It is not merely a clever intellectual exercise. It is the way we distinguish between how things seem to us and how they really are.

All that the Buddha taught depends on grasping the significance of this distinction because it has profound consequences for how you live. Will your life with the myriad beings who share this world be based on understanding or misunderstanding? Will it be based on what's real or what's merely a fantasy about how we think things are?

When You Wonder: Who is Meditating?

Here is another investigation that may seem more subtle because the phenomena you are observing is happening seemingly inside, where you can't "see" it in a palpable way like we can see the blue sky.

Look "inside" at your thoughts just as they occur, without seeking to change or alter them. If your shamatha is stable, you can do this without difficulty. But even if it isn't, you can follow the logic of the vipasyana as you investigate the experience.

When a thought arises, ask: *Is there a thought and a thinker who is separate from the thought, or are the thinker and the thought arising simultaneously so that there is actually no real dividing line between them which can be found anywhere?*

Once your mind has become still through your shamatha practice and you can look at it for longer and longer periods without getting distracted, you begin to train in vipasyana. You do this by experiencing a dissolving of the boundary between what you imagine as the one who is having the experience and the experience that he or she is having.

Another way of practicing the same investigation is to look again at the witness, the one who isn't caught up in thoughts during shamatha. Then this vipasyana practice can occur:

> When you look into who this witness is, can you find
> anybody? Look for the meditator. Look for him or her
> as someone that you think is separate and real. What

is his shape? What is his color? Where is her location? Look and look, but all you will find is another thought or cluster of thoughts. All you will find of that "witness" is a label, a thought-description that reassures you *I'm in here meditating right now.* But the question persists: Who is in there meditating, and where is she?

This is a powerful method of practicing vipasyana, which flogs the mind with this question until it gives up on trying to find anything continuous, solid, real, and existent.

All the teachings in Dharma about enlightenment, awakening, and liberation are based on developing confidence in your inability to locate a self and stabilizing your recognition of this. The more you open yourself to these flashes of sudden intelligence, the more effortlessly they will keep coming to you, and the more deeply you will know the path of awakening as a direct, personal experience, rather than merely a marvelous rumor from books. Here's a wonderful poem about this from Walt Whitman:

Have you practiced so long to learn to read?
Have you felt so proud to get at the meaning of poems?
Stop this day and night with me and you shall possess
the origin of all poems,

You shall possess the good of the earth and sun,
(there are millions of suns left.)
You shall no longer take things at second or third hand,
Nor look through the eyes of the dead,
nor feed on the specters in books,
You shall not look through my eyes either,
nor take them from me,
You shall listen to all sides and filter them
through yourself.[28]

CLARIFYING QUESTIONS ABOUT INSIGHT PRACTICE

Is it true that if you fully engage the practice of shamatha, then the realization of vipasyana will naturally follow?

I think it depends upon how attached you get to shamatha. It's true that vipasyana can naturally arise out of stabilizing shamatha, but the potential problem there—which is referred to a lot in the Tibetan tradition—is that shamatha can bring you to powerful but temporary meditation experiences that you mistakenly interpret as the awakened state. Then you try to deliberately cultivate these experiences again and again, and never realize that they are not the true vipasyana.

These experiences are described as *bliss, clarity,* and *non-thought.* All of them occur when your mind has become very calm and your body very relaxed as a result of shamatha. But because you're holding on to these experiences in a subtle way, there's still fixation going on. As long as you're clinging to your meditation experiences, your awareness is not fully free and not really wide open.

On the other hand, you could have a genuine vipasyana experience without ever having practiced shamatha at all. It would probably be very brief, and without an understanding of its significance, the experience ultimately wouldn't help you that much.

In fact, all of this highlights the whole issue of spiritual materialism once again. You tend to fixate on the "high" of meditation experiences, instead of appreciating that real meditative accomplishment leads to a very grounded, open state of being which eventually becomes very ordinary. My teacher called it "extraordinarily ordinary." He also called it "no big deal."

You talked about flogging the mind with questions until it gives up the search for a self. Flogging *seems like a very aggressive term to apply to something as gentle and nonaggressive as meditation. Could you explain this seeming contradiction?*

The method here is more of a persistent, sharp analysis of the way you habitually think about things. By doing this you use the sharpness of insight to gradually cut through these habits to arrive at an understanding that's closer to how things actually are. The Buddha said that the experience of confusion is based on believing in the way things appear, and the experience of awakening comes from seeing the way things truly are. Vipasyana is the key practice by which you move from the one to the other.

Sharp analysis of our habitual experience is one way of practicing vipasyana. The mind is looking for the mind. We investigate the experience of that mind until we break it down into its smallest constituents and see that there is nothing solid and permanent there. We do that by intellectually pestering our ingrained assumptions about solidity and permanence, in much the same way as a quantum physicist would experimentally reduce seemingly solid matter to its atomic or even subatomic foundations.

Is vipasyana something that you try to do?

In the beginning you do vipasyana practice in the sense that you've studied it and you have an intellectual understanding and you can do some of the exercises that are taught to cultivate the experience of vipasyana. But over time vipasyana becomes more and more of a spontaneously arising experience. When that kind of openness happens, the instruction is just to let it continue until it ends. Don't try to hold on to it because unless you are a Buddha, it will probably end pretty quickly!

One of the greatest Tibetan masters has said that the only difference between an ordinary person and a Buddha is that an ordinary person has flashes of the insight of vipasyana whereas a Buddha has the continuous experience of it. And since the awakened state can't be fabricated or faked or fantasized into permanency, it's obvious that whatever method there might be to encourage that continuous experience must be connected with letting go, relaxing, and opening, rather than trying very hard to make it happen.

An image that one of my teachers has given is: When you hit a gong, the moment when the sound happens is like the glimpse of the awakened state. But then you don't keep hitting the gong. You just let the original sound continue. If you try to hit the gong again and again, then you actually end up pushing the experience further away because of your greed to keep repeating it.

This is described as recognizing and letting be. When you let the spontaneous strike of vipasyana ring out and reverberate into space—and you can simply be present with it until it fades—you've moved from the vipasyana of analysis and investigation to the vipasyana of direct experience. The first is a kind of gateway, but the second is the real thing!

Is vipasyana the intelligence that shows us we really don't exist?

It's more accurate to say that it shows you the *ego* doesn't exist as a solid, continuous identity. But when you understand this, it's not as if you come to the conclusion that there's just an empty, dead blankness there where *you* used to be. On the contrary, discovering that your ego is fiction frees you to understand that you *do* exist in a way that is completely interconnected and interpenetrating with everything and everyone else. Then your life becomes much more of a dance than a struggle. It brings tremendous relief and joy to realize that you don't exist in separation.

My teacher put it much more poetically. He said that you finally understand that you are nothing but a grain of sand with a huge heart.

Is there a danger that realizing we don't exist might cause tremendous anxiety or that it might even cause us to freak out and become psychotic?

The investigations of vipasyana can lead to very profound and groundless experiences. This is precisely why the foundation of shamatha is so important. You have to train first to bring your mind more fully into your body. You have to learn how to sit with difficult psychological material and painful emotions. You have to know yourself in a very grounded way before you can begin to explore yourself in a more groundless way. You have to experience a healthy sense of self before you can experience the freedom of nonself.

Wouldn't it also be quite lonely? Even though we can talk all we want about our interconnectedness, it doesn't seem to take away the loneliness.

The fruitional experience of vipasyana, a sense of interconnectedness, is not particularly a promise that someday you will feel mystical oneness with everyone all the time. The key point is what you just said: interconnectedness doesn't take away loneliness. My own teacher made this point again and again when he talked about the warrior's path. Somehow you experience both your separateness and your connection with others as being two sides of the same coin. They don't contradict each other.

Isn't all this something that finally can't be talked about but that you simply have to experience for yourself?

Definitely. There is a chasm between the words and the meaning. Vipasyana also involves a different way of seeing—with the heart rather than the eyes. It's like the Little Prince when the fox says to him that it's only with the heart, not with the eyes, that we truly see things.

When I go to the parking lot later, I will get into my car as opposed to somebody else's. Is there a nondualistic way to choose my car? I mean, there are different cars, and only one belongs to me.

No, you just choose. You know your car, and you choose your car, but you don't get hung up on the fact that it's not somebody else's car. It's just your car. Nonduality doesn't mean that the individuality of things, and the precise distinctions between things, is no longer there.

I think the more potent issue under the surface here is your sense of ownership, as with "my" car. It gets sticky—this sense of owning things. Of course, it *is* your car, but what we're looking at is the stickiness of that, which comes from forgetting that all of it is merely temporary.

One way to overcome that stickiness of the sense of ownership that I wouldn't necessarily recommend is to have an automobile accident. I once had a bad one, and when I saw the car a few days later, it was just a twisted piece of metal. I didn't have any pride of ownership anymore at all.

Is there a difference between the insights gained through vipasyana practice and the insights that come through psychedelic substances?

The second is not nearly as grounded. In the psychedelic experience there is an exaggerated sense that what you're experiencing is a big deal. The insights come as if they are flashes of light, and you are almost blinded by the light because the insights come to you so quickly. There is a sense of *Wow, wow, yeah, yeah!* But eventually it just becomes mental speed and addiction to what you imagine is peak experience.

It's like the joke about cocaine: "I really love cocaine. It makes me feel like a new man. Trouble is, then the new man wants some too." You keep trying to recreate an experience or an insight rather than patiently cultivating some kind of realization. At some point the experiences become stale and fabricated. You're purely surviving on your memory, and you dull your wakefulness rather than deepening it.

The power of these things is that they may open your eyes to a much bigger world than you previously knew existed, which initially can be very inspiring. This has been true for many people. But at some point you have to face yourself more nakedly.

BITTERSWEET IMPERMANENCE

From the Buddha's vipasyana experiences, he arrived at many core insights that we will explore in the coming chapters. In the teaching on the marks of existence, the Buddha presented a very penetrating and all-encompassing view of life. This view provides a foundational ground for us to later experience his teachings about enlightenment and liberation. It is important to start with how you experience things now rather than base your path to enlightenment on wishful thinking.

The word *mark* points to a quality or characteristic of something which is so inherent to it, so embedded in its nature that if the mark were to be removed, then the thing it was part of would no longer exist. An example of this would be to say that the mark of fire is to burn. This is the essential function of fire; this is its identifying quality, its defining characteristic. Without burning, you would no longer have what we call fire.

In this sense a mark can be seen as something indelible on the phenomenon it describes—like a birthmark, a tattoo that you can't remove, or the permanent ink your mother used to write your name in your underwear when you went away to summer camp. So the mark is something you can't get rid of; you can't escape it.

With the three marks of existence, the Buddha was not describing concepts or ideas or opinions about the phenomenon of existence. Rather he observed these marks as inherent aspects of it that he perceived directly through his vipasyana. They are the living truth, the "is-ness" of our experience, so to speak.

The phenomenon that is being looked at in these teachings was described by the Buddha as *existence*. It's important to understand what existence means in this context. It refers to the experience of human life at its deepest inner core. The marks describe what that depth of experience really consists of. So he used *existence* in somewhat the same way that the modern Western existentialists used it, as a term that invokes the most fundamental conditions under which we live our lives as individual human beings—the unalterable givens of being alive.

The Buddha taught that there are three marks of existence. The first is *impermanence;* the second is *suffering;* the third is *egolessness.* In the next three chapters, we will examine each of these in turn, but in the big picture they are not really separate things. Rather they are three ways of describing the same thing. In one analogy, if existence were a harmonic chord, the three marks would be the three individual but simultaneous notes that made up the chord, and without each of the three notes there would be no chord. As you read about the three marks in detail, you might let yourself reflect on their inseparability. Describing them separately is just a conceptual convenience.

CHANGE OVER TIME

The superficial meaning of impermanence is just "change." It is the perception that everything changes. It is the old adage that "change is the only constant" or "the only thing that doesn't change is change itself." Change is the essential condition for our experience of linear time altogether. Time comes into being only because of the mark of impermanence.

You can observe this in your life in obvious ways and in subtle ways. Each of us can come up with innumerable personal examples of it. One shocking experience of change I had was driving from the airport in Denver to Boulder after an absence of ten years. If you have ever made that drive, the front range of the Rocky Mountains is ahead of you the whole time, and the outline of the peaks is majestically familiar. It is also reassuring in the way it seems never to change. But the land on either side of the highway was now covered with thousands of houses, built very close together as if marching across the plain, and of course there were more gas stations and fast food restaurants and whatnot. The air was also filled with a brownish haze.

The experience was so shocking because I still had a vivid mental image of the landscape as miles of ranches and uncut grasslands with the wind blowing through them, filled with flowers, with the snow-capped mountains lifting into pristine blue air. Just ten years had passed. Shocking.

AGING

Another obvious experience of impermanence might be seeing a relative or friend again after a long time of not seeing him, and you don't immediately recognize him or you have a little shock in recognizing him because he's older and looks different than you remember. The deeper message in moments like these is that you have been holding an image of the person as he was when you last saw him. That image must reconfigure itself in order to synchronize with the reality of the present moment. Of course, he is probably experiencing you in a similar way. The still subtler message is that this aging process has been proceeding imperceptibly from moment to moment, both in your friend and in yourself, since the last time you saw each other. This process is so subtle and imperceptible on a daily basis that you don't notice it, and of course you don't really want to notice it, which helps you not see it.

There is also the subjective shift in how change is experienced as you grow older—a commonly reported and agreed-upon phenomenon. The days of childhood seem to take forever, but in middle age they seem to pass by very fast indeed. This is perhaps especially true in our society, whose whole ethic is built upon a sense of speed, or what one Tibetan teacher called "hurry sickness." As one fifty-five-year-old comic put it, "It seems like fifteen minutes pass, and now it's time for breakfast again."

DEATH

Fifteen years ago I stood in a beautiful meadow in Vermont with my father, who was then eighty-two years old, at the spot where Chögyam Trungpa had been cremated in 1987. Both of us witnessed this event, and I said to my father, "Twelve years have passed since the cremation, yet it feels as if it just happened." And he replied, "Frank, it feels like just yesterday that I was a boy running through meadows like this, chasing butterflies." Two years later, my father too was gone.

RITUAL CHANGE

Sometimes the reality of impermanence is actually reassuring. This is especially true of the cycles of nature that we experience in the changing of the seasons. For example, in autumn the air is cooler, the leaves of the trees blaze with many colors, and your senses are heightened and invigorated. There is also the familiarity of the autumns you have experienced often in the past. This combined sense of freshness and familiarity is very heartening. It is the essential experience of *ritual* in the best sense of that word: something you repeat but, rather than being stale, is fresh each time you repeat it.

The Buddha's insight about impermanence emphasized, however, that for each of us individually the process of change is moving in the same inexorable direction. To paraphrase one of his oral instructions to his students:

> Monks, all composite things are impermanent and subject to decay. Whatever has been put together will eventually fall apart. The end of all meeting is parting, and the end of all birth is death.[29]

ALL THINGS BEGUN, END

This description of impermanence is similar to the second law of thermodynamics, the law of entropy, which sees the universe as being like a great clock that is in the process of running down until it inevitably stops. Of course the uncompromising simplicity of this is something all of us have a very difficult time accepting—a point we will explore further in our discussion of the other two marks. But two brief, closely related examples will make this clearer.

One is the feeling that occurs when you hear about a disaster that has taken the lives of many people, especially when you don't know them personally. It is the common experience of subtle relief or reassurance that you are still alive in the midst of your other feelings of shock and sympathy. The fact that the truth of impermanence has visited others with such force is something that—by an odd twist of reasoning—you make into a reassurance about your own invulnerability and your own permanence.

The other is invoked by a memorable quotation from the Hindu epic *The Mahabharata,* in which one of the main characters responds to the question, what is the greatest wonder in the world?

"The greatest wonder in the world," he replies, "is that with all the death happening everywhere around us every day of our lives, we still believe that it won't happen to us, and live as if it won't."[30]

The last words of the Buddha himself were a teaching on impermanence, when he said to his monks as he lay dying beneath the sal tree: "Now, monks, I am about to die, because as I have taught, all composite things are impermanent. You must be a lamp unto yourselves, and work out your own liberation with great diligence."

Impermanence is the first of the three marks, and it is undeniably difficult and threatening to look at it straightforwardly. On one hand it is essential for developing a courageous attitude that we are able to look directly at this and contemplate it until its reality sinks in and we take it to heart. In the Tibetan tradition, the truth of impermanence is a daily reminder for practitioners about the urgency of exerting oneself on the path of liberation. On the other hand, it is helpful to keep your sense of humor and your compassion about just how difficult this is for any of us to do. For the most part we are unlikely to look at impermanence unless and until it is forced upon us by the circumstances of our own lives. Interestingly, this attitude of humor and compassion about your own denial is part of being a warrior as well.

THE LEVITY AND BLESSING OF IMPERMANENCE

Finally, and as an aspect of that attitude of humor and compassion, we should also remember the positive side of impermanence, expressed eloquently by the Vietnamese Buddhist master Thich Nhat Hanh. He points out that it is only because of impermanence that you are not condemned to be stuck in your negative emotions forever, nor are you condemned to experience the suffering that is the karmic consequence of these negative emotions forever, either.

Because of impermanence, you can grow in your understanding of the Dharma, and you can free yourself from what formerly bound you through the strength of your study and practice. Therefore, as Thich Nhat Hanh says, "Long live impermanence!"[31]

NECESSARY AND
UNNECESSARY SUFFERING

The second mark of existence is suffering. The Sanskrit word for suffering is *dukha*. This word has been translated in various ways—as pain, dissatisfaction, struggle, hassle and inconvenience, and perhaps most powerfully as existential anxiety. This range of definitions is actually quite accurate and very helpful, because it points our attention toward the fact that there are many ways in which you actually experience dukha.

OUR MOST BASIC LEVEL OF SUFFERING

First there is *basic, all-pervading suffering,* which arises from your choiceless experience of impermanence. And this suffering has four aspects: birth, sickness, old age, and death. You may recall three of the four sights which Siddhartha Gautama, the future Buddha, encountered when he escaped his father's palace to see the real world: the sick man by the road, the old man walking painfully along, and the corpse being carried to the cremation ground on the riverbank.

Existential hassle, or inconvenience, is the struggle inherent in how impermanence happens to each of us. It is the basic limitation of being born into a human body. Although for each of us it may unfold on different timetables and with different degrees of apparent grace or awkwardness, it unfolds in the same fundamental way. Your body—no matter how strenuously and conscientiously you pamper it, care for it, nourish it, and fortify it—eventually will fall apart.

Birth

Conventionally, birth expresses the continuity of life and is therefore always a cause for celebration to the family, the clan or the community. But the Buddha taught that for the subjective experience of each individual, birth is an expression of separation and once the umbilical cord is cut, a journey begins that must be made alone.

Death

Death itself here is not just the inevitable, final physical kind, but it is also the way the impermanence is experienced from moment to moment when you are really paying attention. The message of death is that you cannot really hold onto anything in your experience because it keeps shifting. It is fundamentally fickle and uncertain, despite the sense of predictability, repetition, routine, and habit that comprise the general atmosphere in which your daily life is lived. This dance of birth and death on the moment-to-moment level is continuous. It is the reality of working with a constant sense of challenge presented by new situations and the reality of not being able to hold on indefinitely to old situations. This fickle, shifting energy tends to keep you off balance and constantly readjusting or changing in order to maintain balance.

Old Age

One of the defining characteristics of old age is that you are less and less able to maintain your balance in the midst of the fickleness and uncertainty. The momentum of change becomes too confusing and threatening, so you take refuge in predictable routines, nostalgic memories, or inflexible opinions. The truth of old age is poignant and devastating—whether you experience it yourself or see it in someone dear whom you remember as vital and strong.

Sickness

One way of seeing sickness from this point of view is that the stress of riding this energy eventually overwhelms you, and you get off the relentless merry-go-round for a while and boycott its momentum until you're ready to ride it again. Of course the truth of sickness also gives you little reminders all the time—even when you catch a mild cold—that your bodily life is not an invulnerable fortress that you can maintain indefinitely against all internal and external threats.

SUFFERING OF BEING DISCONNECTED FROM WHAT YOU WANT

Generally, the *suffering of alternation* occurs because of the disconnection between what you want and what the world has to offer. It could be the dissatisfaction of not getting what you want in life. It could be the disappointment of losing what you have and are attached to. Perhaps most painfully of all, it could be the experience of getting what you want but then later not wanting it anymore.

You lose your job and can no longer make your house payments and have to sell it. You not only don't get the job you wanted so badly, but someone else you know does get it. The stock market crashes and wipes out your retirement nest egg. Your lover rejects you just when you thought everything was going so well. You yourself fall out of love, and telling the truth to your partner is so painful that you engage in deception. Or else you are brave enough to tell the truth and then experience the empty-heartedness of being alone again, but older. Or you simply get bored with what used to fascinate and entertain you, and you drop it from your life.

This fickleness is part of your psychological response to the underlying fickleness of impermanence. As the unfolding of impermanence occurs on a direct, somatic level, you grasp at its highlights. You look for ways to perch comfortably and happily in the midst of this flow, and occasionally you succeed for a while. But this process too is subject to impermanence, whether because of the fickleness of external circumstances that you cannot control or the fickleness of your own internal process of longing and dissatisfaction.

This dance between desire and dissatisfaction is at the root of the suffering of alternation. You hope again and again that your recurrent and unceasing desire can be satisfied by some object outside of you, but in the long run, or the short run, this hope for satisfaction contains the seeds of its own frustration.

This search for fulfillment in something external to you is (as we've discussed in an earlier chapter) the underlying psychology of materialism. By clinging to any pleasure or comfort in life, you are grasping at what by its very nature will eventually either slip through your fingers or else simply exhaust its ability to satisfy you.

STRUGGLING AGAINST SUFFERING

The accumulated impact of all this frustration ultimately leads to *the suffering of suffering*. Your struggle makes the whole thing more painful still. It is here that the sense of dukha as existential anxiety comes fully into play. In your struggle to relate to the ongoing experience of hassle, longing and dissatisfaction, you begin to panic. You begin to feel that you are losing the game of life, and that it is the only game there is.

Sartre wonderfully titled one of his plays *No Exit*. Just like his characters, you have a vague but growing realization that there seems to be no way out of this cycle and that you are running out of time. You defend against this growing sense of disillusionment and panic by becoming more and more armored and careful, cynical, less vulnerable and less spontaneous. You retreat into a posture of denial. You fortify your cocoon like a psychological fallout shelter.

This inner defensiveness, this gradually increasing tightness in your state of being and the insensitivity and numbness that accompany it, strengthens the walls of your self-created prison. It also ironically accelerates your aging. So it is a kind of vicious circle.

This is the predicament that the Buddha saw as universal for human beings. It begins with the truth of impermanence and proceeds through your increasingly complex and defensive strategies to manipulate, avoid, or outwit it—all of which are doomed to fail. And the more cleverly and energetically you try to find a way out, the more you actually intensify your experience of suffering.

ACCEPTING THE HARD TRUTHS

When life is seen in this way, it is rather stark—and at first undeniably depressing. Historically, this teaching initially gave Buddhism a reputation among Western scholars for being gloomy and depressing. But the truth of the matter is that it is depressing only from the wishful and self-deceiving perspective of the ego. If you experience this kind of depression, it can actually be a valuable wake-up call for you. It might prod you to begin to have some curiosity about how you came to be caught in such a seemingly airtight trap.

From the point of view of the warrior—or a Buddha-in-progress, if you will—this view of life is sobering, accurate, and realistic. It is an inspiration to look further, to find out more. This is what the Buddha did, and you could do the same.

The Buddha's first teaching after his awakening that life is suffering is worth exploring here because it is significant to appreciate that Buddha taught about suffering in these two ways: as a mark of existence and as a Noble Truth. The first is clinical and offers a diagnosis of our basic problem, and the second is inspirational and offers the freedom that results from acknowledging how things are.

He called it a "noble" truth. He didn't call it the first lousy truth, or trivial truth, or insulting truth, or depressing truth. Why is this? Perhaps because he wanted to communicate that if you are willing to go into the suffering with enough openness, bravery, honesty, and curiosity, then the suffering has tremendous richness, and a tremendous amount to teach you about how to live as a genuine human being. If you can finally stop evading, ignoring, denying, or sugar coating this truth and stop entertaining yourself continually in order to pretend it isn't there, you can finally stop altogether, look directly at it, take it completely to heart, and recognize that it applies not only to you but to all others who share this world with you. Then, and only then, the recognition of its truth could lead you to liberation and to a deeper compassion. But you must let go of the delusion of your specialness and drop the defenses and concepts that separate you from others and from life altogether.

By recognizing shared suffering, you might glimpse the possibility that all of life is your family, not just those in your immediate family who are near and dear to you. In this way, your appreciation of the truth of suffering can become a gateway to a much larger, richer experience of your life.

23

Revolutionary Egolessness

The third mark of existence is the mark of nonself—also called non-ego, or *egolessness*. Of all the discoveries of the Buddha's practice of vipasyana, this was perhaps the most revolutionary.

There is an important distinction between the "ego" of Western psychology and the "ego" of Buddhist psychology. The first, as discussed briefly in chapter 13, is considered a necessary function, while the second is considered an unnecessary mistake. Freud's own revolutionary insight was into the tension between conscious and unconscious processes of the mind—especially between the conscious ego and the unconscious, instinctual id. The Buddha also concerned himself with conscious and unconscious mental processes, but it would be more accurate to use the terms *unaware* or *not-knowing* to describe what the Buddha meant by "unconscious."

To the Buddha, ego encompasses the entire landscape of confusion. He would have seen all of the processes identified by Freud—no matter how unconscious they are or how much you've brought them into your awareness—as the functioning of ego. In this more global sense, the Buddha saw ego as a fundamental, dualistic confusion about your relationship with the world. This dualistic confusion is your underlying belief that the subjective experience of yourself—the "I"—and the world you perceive "out there" are two separate realities, each with its own independent existence. Through his penetrating vipasyana, the Buddha saw that this dualistic perception was a profound distortion of how things really are. He also saw that this distortion is kept alive through endless mental and emotional grasping and fixation, and that as long as you continue to believe that your dualistic version of the world is real, you are unconscious in the deepest sense. And you suffer.

In order to avoid confusing Freud's definition of ego and the Buddha's definition of ego, when describing what the Buddha discovered in looking deeply at the suffering mind, I will use the term *ego-fixation*. Ego-fixation is the process of repetitive mental constructions that keep rebuilding themselves (and collapsing) moment after moment in order to keep reinforcing your belief that the dualistic separation between yourself and the world is real. These repetitive constructions unfold in a stable pattern that has five components. The Buddha called these the *Five Skandhas.*

HOW EGO-FIXATION GROWS LIKE A TREE

The word *skandha* means "heap" or "aggregate." The traditional analogy is that ego-fixation is like a heap of different particles both coarse and fine, mixed together and then added to water in order to make concrete. The end result is solid, but the components are distinct, and each has its own particular quality. You can also think of the development of the skandhas as growing like a tree.

The Roots of Ignorance/Form

Ego-fixation begins at the roots, deep under the ground. The roots are the first skandha, called *Ignorance/Form.* It is in the first skandha that the mind initially ignores the possibility of openness, free of duality. "Openness" here refers to the Buddha's realization that the mind and what it perceives are not two separate things but are a single, unified field of awareness, or knowing.

According to the Buddha, within the fundamental openness of your awareness, ego-fixation starts as a very deep split, or experience of duality, based upon ignoring that openness. You mistakenly assume that this sense of separation you perceive between yourself and the world all around you, from moment to moment, is ultimately real. So you begin to create an entire world. And you can only maintain this mistaken assumption by ignoring the original, open ground of your awareness over and over again.

In your everyday life, you aren't even in touch with that ignorance anymore; you don't even remember when it happened or that it happened. Unfortunately, this split conditions everything: all of your thinking, all of your painful emotions, and all of your actions arise out of this split that you can't even remember or access for the most part.

In this way, the first skandha is down in the roots and under the ground, because it's unseen. You have ignored the openness of reality and then are no longer aware that you did that and that you keep doing it.

Out of this Ignorance arises Form—the everyday world of subject and object, this and that, "I" and "other." The word *form* points to the fact that what could be an open, fluid, and free experience of life becomes solidified and frozen into a dualistic pattern, like flowing water freezing into immoveable ice. It is then assumed to be ultimately real.

The Trunk of Feeling and Branches of Perception/Impulse

The tree of ego-fixation grows out of the ground and becomes visible, and more and more articulated and complex. You start adding embellishments to the original duality to make it more convincing. As it grows and emerges out of the ground, you experience the second and third skandhas of *Feeling* and *Perception/Impulse*.

With Feeling, the roots of the first skandha become the trunk of the tree. Here you take a primitive stance in relationship to the object—you either want to grasp it, reject it, or pay no attention to it because it holds no interest for you, no emotional charge. Feeling is the primitive experience of "me and my friend," "me and my enemy," "me and something or someone I couldn't care less about and hardly even notice."

When the branches begin to articulate themselves further out of the trunk, you experience the third skandha of Perception/Impulse, in which you begin to act toward the object in a way consistent with your Feeling: drawing it toward you, pushing it away, or screening it out. It's the level of "me wanting to take care of my friend," "me wanting to destroy my enemy," or "me actively ignoring everyone else altogether." This way of perceiving the "other" is impulsive by nature, based as it is on the primitive bias established in the previous skandha of Feeling so that there is no room for clarity or objectivity in the perception itself.

The Numerous Twigs of Concept

When the branches begin to articulate themselves further, you experience the fourth skandha, called *Concept* or *Formation,* in which you begin to attach value judgments to your experience of the object. These value judgments are polarities—good and bad, beautiful and ugly, brilliant and stupid, and so on. It's the level of "me wanting to hurt my enemy because he is bad, ugly, and stupid," or "me wanting to help my friend because of all her wonderful qualities." At this point, you make use of the logic of comparison in order to give your original bias more credibility.

The skandha of Concept is especially powerful because its reliance on logic gives it an intimidating veneer of plausibility. It is as if the more primitive motivations of the second and third skandhas have now been given a respectable cover. Like a lawyer building your case, you now have unassailable reasons for asserting or defending your territorial grip on your world.

The Fluttering Leaves of Consciousness

Finally, from these twigs grow myriad leaves that flutter in the wind. This is the culmination of the process, the fifth skandha, called *Consciousness*. These are all those discursive thoughts and all those little emotional upheavals you experience moment to moment in your meditation practice. A steady rustling sound of thoughts and emotions blowing here and there drones interminably on in your mind throughout the day (and even in your dreams). This is the final stage of this growth of ego-fixation, an elaborate hoax that keeps you from seeing your true nature clearly.

The fifth skandha could also be compared to a congressional filibuster—when a congressman holds the floor indefinitely, even reading the phone book aloud from cover to cover, to prevent a bill he knows he will lose from coming to a vote. At this level of over-complication, you talk endlessly to yourself about your predicament with lover or friend or enemy, spinning story lines of all kinds to create a seemingly solid, airtight narrative of your world and your life. It's your own private *As the World Turns* soap opera.

Growth at Lightning Speed

The Buddha found that this fixated process of complicating your perception happens very fast, which is one of the reasons it is so difficult to expose. To return to the metaphor of mixing concrete, when any experience arises, you collect and solidify and build the five skandhas with lightning speed, at the rate of sixty times per second! It's the inner equivalent of a particle accelerator in nuclear physics.

The key point here is that your ego-fixation is always unconscious and unaware of its own assumption that there's a solid world "out there" separated from your solid world "in here." What keeps the game of ego-fixation endlessly going is this lack of awareness that you are really an open ground free from these conceptual labels and divisions. You are constantly ignoring that open ground.

On the deepest level, ego-fixation is the state of being perpetually unconscious and unaware. The Buddha saw all this clearly and unmistakably through his practice of vipasyana and the knowing that arose from this practice.

THE POWER OF PROJECTION

By being unaware, ego-fixation creates a cramped and limited version of reality based on projection. *Projection* is a fundamental concept in both Buddhist and Western psychology. The derivation of the word from the Latin *jection* means "throw," and *pro* means "forward" or "in front of." The mind is constantly throwing its version of reality in front of itself, as it were, so as not to see clearly what is actually there. It's like putting a veil over someone's face and then seeing only the veil rather than the face that the veil is covering. Projection creates an ongoing misunderstanding and perpetuates a distortion in the way you experience the world. You're constantly seeing things through the filter of your misinterpretation. This is the activity of projection.

It isn't quite accurate even to say that the ego-fixation of the skandhas is *doing* this. Ego-fixation isn't doing the projection; ego-fixation *is* the process of projection itself. That's why we can say that ego-fixation (and therefore the skandhas) doesn't really exist, because there isn't really anything anywhere that is doing this. It's not a *thing*, but rather a *process* that keeps flickering over and over again in the basic openness, like a bad light bulb. But it's so constant and all-pervasive that you are not able to see anything else, so you conclude that it's real.

Ego-fixation is like watching the images on a screen when you go to a movie. At a film, you are watching images being projected on a blank screen, twenty-four images per second. You could stop them at any single place. Do you ever stop your DVD movie because you want to go get something from the kitchen?

Or because the story has become so frightening that you need to break its spell for a moment? Then all the drama that had you in its thrall is just frozen there in a single, isolated frame. When the imaginary sense of continuity is cut, your belief and participation in the illusion instantly collapses.

The world of ego-fixation is just like that. It's like the projection of a film, in that it gives the illusion of continuity and creates a 24/7 suspension of disbelief. You lose track of yourself altogether, even though if you simply stop the projector, the discontinuity of separate images becomes obvious. Therefore, you make your projections reality as a permanent, continuous thing.

THE IMPOSED REALITY OF SUFFERING

While this experience is real, it is not real in the sense of being solid and fixed and unchanging. It is real in the way its vividness affects how you perceive the world, how you experience it and therefore, how you live your life. *Your projections become real in the sense that they lead to suffering. That suffering is the reality of ego-fixation.* No one, not even the most ingenious Buddhist philosopher, will ever be able to tell you that your suffering isn't real. That doesn't work. That's what is so powerful about the truth of suffering in the three marks of existence: you can't use one of the marks in order to escape the other. However, the illusory projected world that causes so much of your suffering is *not* real. It is a fabrication. You make it up, moment to moment.

In Shambhala warrior language, this world that you have created out of your projections in order to give yourself a sense of security is the cocoon. When you practice meditation, you develop more and more curiosity and longing to explore the cocoon, to see through it, and to live a life that is not conditioned by it. You see that what you thought was giving you a sense of security is actually a kind of prison for you.

THE DELIGHTFUL FREEDOM OF EGOLESSNESS

When the teaching on non-ego-fixation or *egolessness* is presented, people tend to get upset and very threatened. In light of this, it is helpful to give a metaphorical example that casts the teaching in a more positive light for you—since it is actually a tremendously liberating experience. Indeed, the Buddha taught that egolessness is the basis of enlightenment.

Living with ego-fixation as your main reference point is like swimming with all your clothes on. You are weighed down, less buoyant, and your movements are restricted. There is also a constant sense of struggle and an underlying fear that you might sink and drown. Letting go of that unnecessary accumulation is like taking off the clothes and swimming naked. You experience the freedom and joy of that simplicity, that lightness, that direct contact with the water. Your anxiety and struggle vanish. Such a relief!

In the beginning you don't experience egolessness that way. You are so accustomed to your self-created little world that any threat to its existence makes you very fearful. Any sudden loss—whether a person, object, or habit—that makes your familiar world shift or feel less solidly real, can bring on a powerful anxiety.

From this point of view, the practice of meditation is to slowly get used to the openness and freedom that comes from not needing to check back to your habitual patterns all the time. What you are doing when you sit and meditate is looking at your mind as if in a laboratory. You are looking at your mind and watching it spin. You begin to see that the way your mind is spinning during meditation practice is precisely the way it spins when you are out in the world, relating to your life. The difference is that during meditation you give yourself the luxurious opportunity to look closely at that mind instead of taking its chatter for granted.

If you look long and deeply enough at your mind, you will discover that it's not what you thought it was. As all the great spiritual traditions say, "the truth will set you free." The truth is that your mind is fundamentally open and free of conceptual limitations. The freedom you experience in meditation results from simply being able to see clearly the ongoing game of fixating on your experience—and then realizing that you actually don't have to participate any longer.

Cultivating this ability takes time. It takes time to become accustomed to openness. It takes time to work through all the fears and emotional reactions that you have about the possibility that there might be a different way to approach your life. But you have time. You still have time. In fact, most of you who are reading this probably have much more time than I do at this point!

Don't waste that time.

BEING FIXATED AND BEING FREE

What's actually happening when you practice shamatha and vipasyana along the path to enlightenment? The Eight Kinds of Consciousness is a very powerful and fairly simple teaching that is like opening the hood of your car and studying the engine so you can see what makes the car stall out and what makes it move down the road.

Rather than thinking there are actually eight separately existing things, instead regard them as eight different ways the mind experiences phenomena. This view helps you approach this teaching as a way to understand how you can go from being bound to being free.

THE FIVE SENSES

The first *five consciousnesses* are the five senses. The teachings on vipasyana in chapter 19 talked about observing how direct perception occurs through your five senses and then how you label what you perceive. Training your mind in direct perception without labels is one way of experiencing vipasyana, or insight into how things really are.

By engaging this training, you begin to understand that there is a real difference between perceiving the world with labels attached to your perceptions and dropping the filter of these labels so that you experience things directly and nakedly. It is like the difference between hanging out with your longtime, good friend and experiencing his presence now versus experiencing your memory of him, frozen in time.

Each of the five senses of seeing, hearing, smelling, tasting, and touching have their own sense organ, of course. But in Buddhist psychology it's not the sense organ itself that experiences sight, sound, smell, taste, and touch. Rather the mind experiences them, and the organs are merely gateways. To illustrate, it's pretty clear that while a corpse has these five sense organs, it does not experience anything.

The experiences that arise from these gateways are called "pure perception." They are called "pure" in the sense that they are immediate and free of any conceptual overlay. Think back to the teaching on *first thought* in vipasyana in chapter 19. These types of perceptions occur before you come up with thoughts or words to describe them.

THE MIND THAT THINKS

Next, there's a *sixth consciousness,* which is generally referred to as "the mind that thinks." It could also be thought of as the logical mind, the reasoning mind, or the dualistic-labeling mind. The fact that it labels experience is not regarded as undesirable or unneeded, but simply as a description of how it functions. In the world, concepts and labels are, of course, essential if you are to communicate with anyone at all. This is the mind that for each sense identifies *I am seeing the blue sky, I am hearing reggae music,* or *I am smelling chopped onions.* It's the mind that knows what it knows. And it is admittedly conceptual; it's not direct, pure perception anymore.

This is dualistic mind. It "takes care of business," as it were, and therefore, it always relates to the world as if the subject-object distinction were ultimately real. The sixth consciousness, then, is akin to how Freud defined the ego: the managerial consciousness we use to cope with the details and challenges of life.

This is also the mind that practices shamatha. The sixth consciousness can be educated about what the object of meditation is, and then knows how to come back to it again and again. In order to keep functioning properly, it can call upon memories of what it previously learned. While this is somewhat mechanical, it is clear and intelligent in being able to function at this level with great efficiency.

STOREHOUSE OF EXPERIENCE

Because the *seventh consciousness* plays such a vital role in linking the sixth and eighth consciousnesses, I will return to discuss it after we have examined the eighth.

The *eighth consciousness* serves as a storehouse or reservoir that holds the traces of all your previous experiences. The difference between the Buddhist understanding of the unconscious and the Western understanding, which is derived from Freud, is that the eighth consciousness holds not just the experience you have inherited from this life you are currently living, but also from previous lives. This is understood to be the only aspect of you that survives or persists from one life to the next.

This reservoir is therefore a huge repository that includes all that you have experienced; the positive and negative imprints these experiences have made on you; and all the information, life lessons, and karmic influences that you have internalized as a result of those imprints. The eighth consciousness is the foundation for perpetuating your past in the form of memory and your future in the form of intentions and expectations. Therefore, it keeps providing you with all the material that you need for this dualistic world to keep reappearing to you and confirming your sense of separateness, as well as all the value judgments and projections that go along with it.

GOSSIPING MIND

The *seventh consciousness* is the connecting link between the eighth, which is latent, and the sixth, which is the conceptual mind through which you actively experience the present moment. My teacher called the seventh consciousness "the mind of subconscious gossip" or the "subconscious nuisance mind." The seventh is a kind of pipeline that keeps drawing material out of the eighth and pumping it, as it were, into the sixth.

The seventh is also called the *klesha* mind. This Sanskrit word means "tortured emotions" or "conflicting emotions" and is used to describe all neurotic thought states that bring suffering. This mind is always busy drawing material from your eighth consciousness and, in effect, interrupting the ability of your sixth consciousness to remain fully present with your experience, whether in meditation or in daily life. This is why at first it is so difficult to practice shamatha. The sixth is trying to rest on the object of meditation, but the seventh keeps interrupting the sixth with distractions from the eighth.

FINDING ENLIGHTENED MIND
IN ORDINARY MIND

The three consciousnesses that arise in the mind (as opposed to the senses) are not actually separate. But because you perceive the world in a dualistic and divided way, you need a model that can clearly explain how that dualistic distortion operates in your daily life and when you are practicing meditation.

The wonderful news is that you can use the framework of this eightfold mind to become enlightened, or simply to progress on the spiritual path. According to Buddhist psychology, you can progress by training the seventh consciousness to break its compulsive habit of activating the eighth. And beyond that, you can attain enlightenment by, as one teacher puts it, convincing the seventh that the eighth is not a self, not an "I" that really exists in a solid and separate and dualistic way.

The result of this two-fold training is that the unconscious imprints of the eighth gradually lose their power to influence our present experience. Over time, all that unconscious material is completely liberated. The process is similar to the analytic journey in Freud's psychoanalysis, where the purpose is to make the unconscious fully conscious. However, there are two crucial differences. Freud's conception of the unconscious does not encompass past lives. And Freud believed the best we could hope for was an uneasy truce between conscious and unconscious minds, whereas the Buddha—and countless masters of the Dharma since—assert that the eighth consciousness can eventually be completely purified, completely liberated.

Liberation occurs when the seventh finally realizes that it has been fooled into assuming that the eighth is a separate, truly existing self. At that point, the dualistic barrier between the seventh and the eighth dissolves, and their inseparability becomes the awakened mind itself.

THE EXPERIENCE OF ENLIGHTENMENT

Despite the fact that the teaching on the eight kinds of consciousness is conceptual, it is a strikingly elegant model that helps you grasp what happens when the mind is freed from fixation into liberation.

In one sense, all of the eight consciousnesses become enlightened at once, in that there are no longer any conflicts or struggles between any of their functions or relationships with each other.

The five senses continue to function in a direct, nonconceptual way. The sixth experiences faultless, still mindfulness; it may at times generate conceptualizations and thoughts but without being distracted or identified with them in the old way. The seventh resolves its confusion about the eighth through the insights of vipasyana. The eighth, which held all the unconscious material from the past, is purified of all those traces and remains as a clear knowing—without any confusion in it any longer. There's no more clinging to an idea of "me" anywhere. At this point the eighth becomes what is traditionally called the Clear Light Awareness, and the practitioner becomes enlightened.

The source of the problem has become the source of the solution.

THE DUALISM OF THE MODERN
SCIENTIFIC APPROACH

When studying this model or the Five Skandhas, some interesting questions may arise for a modern Western person raised with a scientific appreciation of the world. You may wonder whether current discoveries in neuroscience render these ancient models as quaint, or even obsolete. But the models generated by neuroscience are still embedded in a dualistic understanding of the mind. While these models have a great deal to tell us about the connection between neurological processes and mental and emotional states and are very useful for treating psychological disorders, they rely on the scientific method, which is a dualistic, cause-and-effect viewpoint.

As a result, these models do not yet account for the nondual experience that has universally been understood as the basis for the awakened state. These models may give us more tools to manage our confusion and disease, but they do not provide the tools to set us free.

AGNOSTIC APPROACH TO REBIRTH

Implicit in the description of the eighth consciousness is the doctrine of rebirth, which may inspire questions. Many Asian cultures that housed Buddhism believe in reincarnation or rebirth, or the conviction that there must be something in the very essence of us that continues from life to life and cannot die. While many Western people are deeply drawn to Buddhist theory and practice, not all believe unquestioningly in rebirth.

While the traditional model of the eight kinds of consciousness sees the eighth as that which continues from one life to the next, we also have this intriguing teaching from the Buddha. He told his monks that even if there were no past and future lives, if they practiced in the way he instructed them, they would die without fear or regret. For modern Western students of the Dharma, especially those of you who remain agnostic about the existence of past and future lives, this teaching can help you practice wholeheartedly in this life without excessive hope and fear about what may or may not happen in a future life. In doing this, it can strengthen your commitment to cultivating the fearless experience of *nowness* as the foundation for your spiritual path.

THE PAINFUL HALLUCINATIONS OF YOUR DAILY LIFE

I n the teaching on the development of ego-fixation through the Five Skandhas, you saw how the repetitive process of projection works and how it fools you into believing that you really exist in some solid, enduring way. This mistaken belief requires constant reinforcement. It requires a world that keeps giving you messages of solidity, as if you are looking at your reflection in a mirror to make sure you're still there. The reflection is vivid, colorful, and convincing. It feels like home; it feels like "me." You have created a psychological realm that you can live in, and maintaining it is now your full-time occupation.

The Buddha taught that there are six of these realms and that each of them comes into existence through the power of a particular emotion, or *klesha,* which you inevitably experience as painful.

THE EMOTIONS THAT TORTURE YOU

My teacher once said that your emotions are really just thoughts with a lot of energy inside them. The thoughts are ongoing dualistic projects that ask the questions: How am I relating to this situation? How might I be hurt by this situation? How might I gain from this situation?

These are your storylines, your personal soap operas. Kleshas are constantly fueled by this compulsive relationship that "I" have with all my experiences. You use them to protect this sense of "me," to keep it in business day and night. Because you are completely identified with the storyline *"What about me?"* you are unable to work skillfully with the energy that drives it.

When the energy of a klesha becomes so powerful and so habitual that it affects your whole way of relating to your life and generates the ongoing environment for all your dealings with the world, it becomes a *realm.* It is like a play you are wholeheartedly acting in without ever remembering it is merely a play. In the Tibetan Buddhist tradition, these negative emotions and the realms they create are described in two ways: as literal and as psychological.

The psychological understanding of the realms is probably more accessible (and acceptable) to us in the modern Western world. Psychologically, the realms are states of emotional fixation that you cycle in and out of constantly. What this means is that, though you have literally taken birth as a human being, at the same time you have the potential to become subject to the kleshas of all the other realms. As a result, you can create worlds within your human life that have many of the characteristics of the other five realms. It's useful to think of these realms as the styles with which you interior decorate your *cocoon,* where you live inside a world you built from your projections. Whether living in there is painful or pleasurable, you find it preferable to the process of shedding your emotional armor and coming out into the open space of warriorship.

HOW EGO-FIXATION CREATES
THE WORLD YOU EXPERIENCE

The six realms are closely linked to the Five Skandhas, and as a result also have three basic energetic styles: you can draw your projections toward you because of your attraction to them, you can push them away because of your aversion to them, or you can ignore them altogether because of your lack of interest in them. Passion, aggression, and ignorance are also called the *three poisons* because they are toxic to your basic sanity and your ultimate happiness.

In the development of the Five Skandhas, it is in the second and third skandhas of Feeling and Perception/Impulse that this toxic relationship begins to take root. You have developed a primitive relationship with the fundamental dualistic projection you created originally in the first skandha of Ignorance/Form. Next, you perceive it as friend, enemy, or neutral—and after that you either draw it in, push it away, or ignore it completely.

It is on this primitive foundation that you build the realms. The underlying bias and territoriality of the second and third skandhas is reinforced by the fourth and fifth skandhas' logical categories and persuasive storylines. The realms themselves occur during the fourth and fifth skandhas—Concept and Consciousness. This is the conscious level where the game of ego-fixation has become more precise, more articulated, and more visible. It is this level that is most accessible to you in meditation practice, because it is the level at which you can most clearly hear yourself endlessly repeating the story of your life and your personal world and telling yourself why it has to be the way it is.

VARIETIES OF EXPERIENCE AND THE NATURE OF PROJECTION

While reading the descriptions of these realms in the next chapter, it is important to keep in mind that from a psychological perspective, the realms are states of fixation that all human beings experience at one time or another. You cycle in and out of these states all the time but tend to be more drawn to one than the others based on your karmic inheritance and habitual patterns.

Altogether, the six realms create a psychological environment that pervades your waking life, not to mention your dreams. In fact, you can relate to any theme or issue in your life from within the perspective of one of the six realm mentalities.

Traditional Tibetan teachings express this insight by using an analogy of water. A being in each of the six realms experiences water in a unique way. For humans, water is something to drink that satisfies thirst. For hungry ghosts, water is something to drink that never satisfies anything. For fish (an animal) water is something to live in, for jealous gods it is something precious to keep others from having, and for gods it is transcendent nectar to derive pleasure from. For hell beings, water is experienced agonizingly as molten iron. This teaching is a potent reminder that rather than being a solid thing "out there," the phenomenal world is made out of your projections.

Because the realms depend entirely on projections of a certain kind to create the level of fixation through which they can maintain themselves, they are shifty. Interestingly, this shifty play of perception is a further demonstration of the Buddha's teaching on egolessness. Your inner world and its reflection in the world outside just don't exist as solid separate entities—they are purely the product of the mind's projections.

THE EMOTIONAL REALMS IN RELATIONSHIP

You can enter into different realms depending upon whom you are hanging out with or what social environment you are relating to—a further demonstration of the egoless aspect of experience. No doubt you are familiar with the experience of feeling like a slightly different person in varying scenarios and company. Because ego-fixation doesn't exist as a solid, continuous thing, the mind is free to shift in and out of projections of different kinds, and these projections tend to be reinforced by the projections that are coming back from "the other out there." This dance of relationship, also known as "interconnectedness" is the fundamental experience you continually have. In this sense, you mutually create the realms with others.

Mind can be fixated, yet fickle at the same time. As soon as you leave a particular psychological environment, your mind may be freed from the mentality you were so caught up in. From the point of view of practice, such experiences can serve as reminders that, although you may have temporarily escaped the intense power of an environment that activated a particular "torturous emotion" in you, the seeds for that painful distortion are still present in your mind. They can only be fully uprooted by the gradual, gentle application of warrior practice.

THE LITERAL EXISTENCE OF THE REALMS

Many Tibetan masters describe these realms in a very matter-of-fact way as actual places. They teach that, as human beings, most of us can see only the inhabitants of the human and animal realms. We can't see the others, they add, because of karmic limitations on our vision, but there are also beings that literally inhabit the realms of hell, hungry ghosts, gods, and jealous gods.

My own teacher taught this material to Western students from a purely psychological perspective because he understood that this was the way we could relate to the subject. But if you pressed him about it, he would sometimes describe his own perception of beings in these realms as literal manifestations. He would do this with the same matter-of-factness that you might use to describe the last time you caught sight of your next-door neighbor. So while their literal existence may be a matter of belief—or disbelief—for us, Tibetan masters seem to experience them with direct perception. This ability to perceive beings in other realms directly is said to be one of the accomplishments of the profound realization of vipasyana. Time and again, in the presence of my teachers—especially Chögyam Trungpa—I was made aware, gently but shockingly, of the karmic limitations of my own vision of reality.

THE REALMS OF
EMOTIONAL FIXATION

There are three lower realms and three higher realms. The experiences of the lower realms are more clouded and claustrophobic because the conflicting emotion is so powerful that you are utterly engrossed in it and overwhelmed by it. The higher realms are regarded as more intelligent and less painful—although not that much less painful from the point of view of a Buddha. From a Buddha's perspective, even if the lower realms experience the pain of their conflicting emotions more intensely than the higher realms, what all the realms—without exception—have in common is that they cling to the belief that the "I" truly exists. The Buddha taught that there can be no lasting happiness until that belief is given up.

ANIMALS: DOGGED DETERMINATION

The first of the lower realms is the *animal realm,* which is characterized by ignorance. The psychological mechanism of the animal realm is based on your focus on accomplishing a certain result and paying no attention to the environment around you. There is a lack of panoramic awareness. You are concerned only about achieving your goal, and you simply move toward it until something blocks the way. You have a kind of steamroller sincerity about what you are trying to accomplish, and you are not interested in being told that it can't be done or that there are other ways of doing it.

In the animal realm, the basic concern is survival and enhancing it with a sense of security. You prefer your livelihood to be repetitive, predictable, and somewhat mindless. You would like cradle-to-grave security and want as few surprises as possible. There is little or no sense of humor and therefore, no potential to see your seriousness and relax a little. We laugh about something because we suddenly see it in a new way, as happens in an "aha!" experience. But the ability to laugh at ourselves is an expression of intelligence and the animal realm is too gullible, too serious. Because you are completely identified with what you want to accomplish, if you don't accomplish it, you experience tremendous disappointment.

These qualities are what my dear, departed little Scottish terrier Magic expressed while waiting for his dinner. For nearly fourteen years—from the time he was a tiny pup—I fed him every night, which adds up to about four thousand feedings. But every single night of his life, he would come into the kitchen and sit there with great intensity, waiting anxiously to be fed, fearing it might not happen. Nothing would deter him from this stubborn insistence.

HELL: A CLOSED LOOP OF ANGER

The *hell realm,* which is characterized by the aggression of anger and hatred, is the most painful of the realms because of its relentless claustrophobia. This claustrophobia inevitably accompanies your aggression because the tension and tightness make you unable to find any sense of psychological space or relaxation. The experience contains a Catch-22 because the very claustrophobia of the anger makes you lash out in order to relieve yourself of it. And when you lash out at your world, the world responds in kind. Your projections bounce back on you because receiving the hatred is equally painful for others. It is like a hot potato that they don't want to hold any more than you do. This simply intensifies your own anger and hatred further. You are caught in an endless no-win situation, a self-fulfilling loop of conflict—like the politics of the Middle East. As Gandhi memorably said, "An eye for an eye makes the whole world blind."

Here are some portrayals of how this works:

- In the classic Christian epic *The Divine Comedy,* Dante's description of the nine circles of hell is unbearably painful precisely because there is no escape.

- In Sartre's play *No Exit,* he said, "Hell is other people." The Buddha would probably find Sartre's famous closing lines a bit too pessimistic. The Buddha would revise it to "Hell is my experience of anger and hatred toward other people."

- Recall the film *War of the Roses,* where the no-exit momentum of resentment and hatred between the husband and wife drives them mercilessly to a horrific conclusion.

- In the physical and psychological environment of a maximum-security prison, both prisoners and guards participate together in a closed loop of fear and aggression with no real relief. At this point, the psychological claustrophobia of anger and hatred has become visibly externalized in an environment that reflects it in every excruciating detail.

All the world's spiritual traditions invariably describe hell as intense cold or intense heat. Either the anger and hatred freeze you so that you are unable to communicate with the world, to soften and play with it in any way, or else it burns you because the intensity of your pain is so great that it becomes all consuming. Robert Frost put it succinctly and poignantly in the poem *Fire and Ice:*

> Some say the world will end in fire,
> Some say in ice.
> From what I've tasted of desire,
> I hold with those who favor fire,
> But if it had to perish twice,
> I think I know enough of hate
> To say that for destruction ice
> Is also great, and would suffice.[32]

HUNGRY GHOSTS: DESIRE THAT NOTHING SATIATES

The third of the lower realms is called the *hungry ghost* realm and is characterized by insatiable hunger or desire. It is a passion that grasps at things without relief or perspective or resourcefulness. In this realm, you are propelled by a sense that the world has endless delights that you can't have or enjoy, while others can. There is an immense poverty mentality because you believe that while there is so much richness and abundance all around, you are somehow condemned always to be separated from it. You are like a child pressing her nose against the window of FAO Schwarz toy store. Your whole relationship to your life is based on this poverty and hunger. The Catch-22 in this realm is that even if you get what you want, having it does not satisfy you because you are so consumed by the desire itself. It's as if desire has become your full-time occupation. This is why the hungry ghost mentality is at the root of all addictive behaviors.

In the iconography of Tibetan Buddhist art, the hungry ghost is depicted as a being with a very tiny mouth, a thin neck, and a huge belly. The huge belly symbolizes an all-consuming appetite, but the tiny mouth and thin neck symbolize that there is no way for that belly to ever be filled. The advertising industry makes it their mission to reinforce our hungry ghost sense of dissatisfaction by perpetuating the myth that endless consumption is the true aim of life.

GODS: BLISSING OUT OF TOUCH

The three higher realms are considered more desirable to live in than the lower ones because their relationship to the emotional states that propel them is less desperate, more intelligent and resourceful, and—especially in the case of the *god realm*—more pleasurable.

The god realm creates and sustains itself by dwelling on pleasure. This pleasure can be material, as found in Beverly Hills and the lifestyles of the rich and famous, or it can be a spiritual practice promising endless love, light, and bliss without any sacrifice or discomfort. Sustaining this is based upon a subtle kind of ignorance—much more subtle than the ignorance of the animal realm. In the god realm, you are ignoring all the subtle messages that this realm is not solid and that this pleasure is not going to last forever. You are ignoring the truth of impermanence and instead dwelling on a kind of complacent pride, a smugness of having accomplished something everyone else would like to have.

This realm reflects your preference for pleasure and your desire to maintain it at all costs for as long as possible. It is your seeming good fortune to maintain pleasurable states for a while. Because this is an extremely seductive realm, we would all be dishonest if we pretended we didn't experience some longing to be there now and then. But sooner or later, impermanence intrudes, just as it did in the film *Sunset Boulevard* for Norma Desmond: a desperate, aging starlet from the extinct silent film era. The residents of the god realm must sooner or later face the harsh reality that their beauty, their glamour, their status, and their fame cannot be maintained indefinitely in the face of the constant change within them and all around them. The fall from the god realm is a very long, hard fall.

Recall the life of the Buddha, who was raised in a god realm situation of great wealth and luxury. His life was insulated and protected from the harsh truth that others less fortunate than him were suffering on a daily basis. His awakening began when he ventured outside his palace walls and saw how the other 99 percent lived. Because of his own intelligence and potential for compassion, he recognized that these harsh experiences were not something that he should flee from. Rather, he needed to move toward them and find out more about them.

Traditionally, it is said that there are actual god realms populated by yogis who dwell in very subtle and profound meditative states. According to the Tibetan tradition, in meditation you can fixate so deeply that you are actually reborn as a god. This is done through a profound accomplishment of shamatha's peaceful abiding, but without the freeing and penetrating insight of vipasyana to wake you up suddenly from your sweet dream.

JEALOUS GODS: SCHEMING TO GET AHEAD

In the *jealous god* realm are beings who want to be gods but can't quite attain that level. They actually become so entertained by competition with each other about getting to the god realm that this in itself becomes their realm. The engine that drives the jealous god realm is the aggression of paranoia, competitiveness, jealousy, and envy. Everything you encounter is regarded as a potential threat or an obstacle you must outmaneuver. It is a constant game of power plays, one-upmanship, and inside information, as found in the political game of Washington, DC, or the financial game of Wall Street. It's the game of skillful, scheming Machiavellian diplomatic types who keep the intrigues of the world going.

The jealous god realm is much more sophisticated than the hell realm because the aggression is more socially acceptable. The jealous gods let others do their dirty work for them and walk away from their own grandiose, destructive schemes without being held accountable for the suffering countless others have endured as a result. Whereas the hell realm projects its hatred in a way that appears utterly tortured, stupid, and gross, in the jealous god realm the hatred has been transformed into diplomacy. Even compassion is regarded as just another strategy. In *The Prince,* Machiavelli writes that the ruler who wishes to consolidate his power should not really possess the qualities of wisdom and compassion but should seem to do so if it will further his own selfish ends. If it will not, he should simply abandon such seemingly noble qualities without a second thought.

HUMANS: THE GIFT OF DISAPPOINTMENT

The *human realm,* which is our very own home, has the basic qualities of heartfelt longing, the intelligent ability to create a world that is reasonably comfortable, and great inquisitiveness about how things are as well as how things work. With that intelligent kind of passion, you want to make the world better. You want to understand how it works. You want to go beyond your isolation and connect with others. You want to get the most you can out of this book you are reading right now. You want to be happy. But your efforts are only partially successful, and you experience disappointment.

This disappointment is actually essential because it motivates you to look for a way out of your predicament and to encounter the wisdom that may help you do so. Because you experience disappointment, the human realm provides you with the possibility of a break or gap in fixation so that you can actually begin to free yourself from confusion. By cultivating your innate intelligence, you can begin to see right through the ways in which you keep yourself imprisoned. You can experience an alternative to the claustrophobia of your cocoon. You can experience a relationship to your projections that is more open and less gullible.

The Buddha taught that this opportunity in the human realm is uniquely precious because it is the starting point of your journey toward inner freedom.

The practice of meditation enables you to make the most of this precious opportunity to get up and walk out of the theatre of the realms and into the clear light of reality. The fact that we are currently embodied together in the human realm, with its unique opportunity to hear the teachings on liberation and put them into practice—and that we can explore this opportunity right now—is considered by Tibetan masters to be an extremely auspicious and precious karmic link with each other and with the Dharma. Needless to say, they urge you not to let this opportunity go to waste. Every time my teachers would say this to me, chills would go up my spine. Even recalling their reminders now—especially as I get older—I experience those familiar chills.

In the next chapter, we will look at the experience of the human realm in depth, focusing especially on why it is traditionally regarded as the optimal realm for liberation from ego-fixation.

TRUTHS THAT REMIND
YOU TO WAKE UP

You will find yourself cycling emotionally from time to time through all of the realms of psychological fixation in your daily life. None of us is exempt from the power of the kleshas—whether anger, addictive craving, bewilderment, self-satisfied pride, or insecure competitiveness. Yet each of us has the great good fortune not to have to be afflicted permanently by any of them. It's like playing Monopoly and drawing the card with a picture of the jail; but it says "Just Visiting."

The human world is basically a realm of passion. It is a healthier kind of passion than the addictive kind that hungry ghosts experience because it is mixed with intelligence and resourcefulness. We are capable of securing what we long for and of enjoying it. But because of the truth of impermanence, nothing can give human beings lasting satisfaction or security. As the Buddha taught, we will inevitably either not get what we want, lose what we prize, or simply find ourselves no longer wanting what we once felt we couldn't live without.

UNHOOKING FROM THE CYCLE
OF FRUSTRATION

Yet it is also characteristic of the intelligence of the human realm that we can detach ourselves from this cycle of frustration and look at it objectively and clearly. This is what the Buddha did and what each of us can do for ourselves. By engaging with clarity and kindness, we can untie the knots of suffering and confusion we ourselves have created.

This is why the Buddha called our suffering a "noble" truth. The other realms do not seem to have the gaps of intelligence and clarity that might enable them to reflect on the futility of their game. The struggle to maintain their kleshas as a solid experience is too overwhelming; somehow they are forced to keep playing the same game, again and again. To them it feels like there is too much at stake to stop.

This recognition of the special opportunity for liberation from these patterns of emotional frustration, which the human realm offers us, is a central teaching in Tibetan Buddhism. There is an intense appreciation for having been born as a human being, rather than in one of the other realms. This is especially so since the literal existence of these realms and the inevitability of rebirth are both taken as self-evident, obvious truths in the Tibetan tradition. Reflecting on the special quality of the human realm—that it gives you the opportunity to free yourself from your self-created suffering—becomes a way to rekindle the inspiration to practice meditation on a daily basis.

RECALLING THAT YOUR HUMAN LIFE
IS A PRECIOUS OPPORTUNITY

This reflection is part of a series of four contemplations—called the Four Thoughts That Turn the Mind Toward the Dharma. These are sometimes referred to simply as The Four Reminders.

The first of the Four Reminders expresses deep appreciation for the rare, good fortune in having been born as a human being. It points to the special opportunity your human birth offers to pursue a truly meaningful purpose.

> First, this precious human body,
> free and well favored,
> Is difficult to gain and easy to lose.
> Now I must do something meaningful.[33]

RECALLING THAT YOU DON'T HAVE FOREVER

The second of the Four Reminders draws your attention to the fact that you don't have endless time to make the fullest use of this precious opportunity. It does this by bringing the first mark of existence—impermanence—vividly to mind.

> Second, the world and its inhabitants
> are impermanent,
> Especially the life of beings is like a bubble.
> Death comes without warning—
> this body will be a corpse.
> At that time only the dharma can help me.
> I will practice it now with exertion.[34]

Impermanence is the law of the universe. Your death is an absolute certainty; only the exact time of its coming is unknowable. At the time of your death, nothing you have built up or accumulated or squirreled away during your life will be of any use to you. Indeed, to the extent that these things have become sources of clinging and attachment, they will actually hinder you. Since the necessity of letting go of clinging and attachment is one of the cornerstones of dharma practice and since at the time of death the need to let go will no longer be a matter of choice for you, there is no time like the present moment to begin changing your attitude.

This emphasis on the importance of contemplating the certainty of your death as a way of inspiring you to a sense of urgency about meditative practice is common to many spiritual traditions. Recall the moment when the Yaqui Indian shaman, Don Juan, tells his apprentice Carlos Castaneda that to become an accomplished warrior, he must make a greater commitment to himself. He must stop both his incessant talking and his "internal dialogue." When Carlos asks him how to do this, Don Juan replies that he should visualize his death sitting always on his left shoulder. This will help him remember that there is no time for idle, frivolous verbal or mental chatter.

The Power of Simplicity

The example Henry David Thoreau lives in his classic book, *Walden,* illustrates a similar theme. His experiment in simple and mindful living, which he conducted for two years in a cabin he built on the shore of Walden Pond, was rooted in the same purity and power of intention that might inspire a young Buddhist monk in the forests of Burma. As Thoreau wrote in the chapter "Where I Lived and What I Lived For":

> I went to the woods because I wished to live deliberately, to front only the essential facts of life, and see if I could not learn what it had to teach; and not, when I came to die, discover that I had not lived. I did not wish to live what was not life, living is so dear.[35]

Thoreau consciously withdrew from the commercial bustle of nineteenth-century New England in order to reflect upon life's deeper meaning and purpose. He discovered that he could live quite beautifully with very few possessions or comforts and that this simplicity afforded him the opportunity to be with himself in a deeper way. From this vantage, he could look at his own life and the lives of his neighbors with both detachment and sympathy.

Not surprisingly, his neighbors regarded him as an odd and eccentric person for doing this. Yet he was content to accept their prejudiced view as part of the challenge that must always face an individual who pursues a life of contemplative simplicity with integrity in the midst of an overwhelmingly materialistic culture.

Thoreau died at age forty-three. He never married. His only living relatives at his death were two maiden aunts. They were proper Bostonian ladies who were quite pious and had come to regard him as the black sheep of the family. It is said that they visited him during his final illness and that as they stood by his bedside, one of them said disapprovingly, "Henry, have you made your peace with God yet?"

He is said to have gently replied, "My dear aunt, I was not aware that God and I had ever quarreled."[36] At the time of his death, the way Thoreau lived had left him with a profound sense of peace.

Traditional Renunciation

This attitude of gentleness and simplicity, and the experience that develops from it, is traditionally called *renunciation*. In the Asian countries where the Dharma has been practiced for well over two thousand years, the practice of renunciation has been connected with following the Buddha's life example. You would renounce the world by becoming a monk or nun or mendicant yogi with few or no worldly possessions and attachments. In Southeast Asia, young practitioners would go to forest hermitages or solitary retreat huts and practice meditation completely apart from the society in which they had been born and raised.

This practice was something that the larger society both sanctioned and supported. It was as if these young spiritual seekers were doing this for everyone. To give monastics and yogis food or patronage or any kind of spiritual support conferred merit on the benefactor and the guarantee of a better rebirth. Therefore, the practice of renunciation was an honored part of the life of the individual and of the larger society supporting his efforts to follow the Buddha's example in as pure a way as possible.

Contemporary Renunciation

In our own culture, if you aspire to follow the Buddha's life example, support for renunciation is not so easily obtained. The materialistic assumptions that Thoreau challenged more than 150 years ago are even more formidable now. There are few, if any, avenues you can formally pursue to renounce the world in a traditional way. As a result, you must find ways to emulate the inner commitment of the forest monk while living in the outer wilderness of the technological world.

Perhaps you make a personal connection with the teachings of Dharma—having heard them, read them, or met an inspiring teacher. As a result of this, you begin to commit yourself to mindfulness practice in a wholehearted way. Slowly your practice may begin to pervade your life. It is as if the Dharma begins to haunt you and you can't escape it. The truth of it is reflected back to you from every direction.

As you contemplate the three marks of existence and let them apply to your experience without evasion or denial, you learn that their reality is inescapable. You can't distance yourself from them by intellectualizing them into neat categories. You cannot help but feel in the core of your heart how things are endlessly shifting and changing. You feel the subtle struggle of constantly maintaining your balance in the midst of this—even when your life is "going well." When at last you feel that you have this delicate balancing act under control, something unexpected happens to pull the rug out from beneath you again.

You tell yourself that, somehow, the fact that ego doesn't exist provides you with an escape from this, as if saying to yourself, *Well, if it's all egoless then it's not really happening to me, is it?* But you find instead that the truth of non-ego makes your experience of the shifting poignancy of things more vivid and more direct than ever. In Tibet, this insight is expressed in the adage that those who are still asleep experience pain like the stroke of a hair across the palm of the hand, while those who are awake experience it like the stroke of a hair across the eyeball.

All of these lessons and insights may not come as sudden, explosive revelations. Rather, they gradually seep into your view of your life; they slowly begin to grow inside you. You begin to feel not only a sense of urgency but also a genuine sadness. Your sadness comes not only from your realization of how much time you have already wasted in your cocoon but at how much time everyone around you continues to waste in perpetuating their collective cocoon—a speedy, distracted world of mindlessness and unnecessary suffering. The practice of freeing yourself individually from unnecessary confusion and suffering is sometimes referred to as "the path of not causing harm to yourself and others."

Renouncing being the cause of harm is an essential aspect of the Buddha's teachings. It is not necessary to literally abandon the world altogether. But in practicing mindfulness until it becomes an integral part of your life, your attention to everything you think, say, and do becomes more and more sensitive and refined. This refinement has a powerful effect on your own life and the lives of all the others with whom you're in relationship.

RECALLING THAT THE WORLD'S CONFUSION BEGINS WITH YOU

This commitment to taking daily responsibility for your own contribution to the world's insanity is expressed in the Third Reminder.

> Third, when my death comes I will be helpless.
> Because of my past karma I must now
> abandon neurotic crime.
> I will always devote myself to virtuous actions.
> Thinking this, every day I will examine myself.[37]

You recognize how much pain and chaos your own actions cause you and others when they are based only on your kleshas. You sense acutely that there is less and less room for indulgence of that kind. Even if others all around you continue to live in this way, you recognize the importance of living your own life differently.

You see clearly that all the confusion and suffering in the world begins with your own mind. This is not to say that you personally take the blame for all that confusion. But you see how choiceless it is to begin by first taking full responsibility for your own contribution to the chaos. My teacher called this "developing confidence in your own sanity before you try to fix the world's insanity." He emphasized that it is a narrow path with no sidetracks and that it requires a purity and strength of intention. Because it also requires courage, it is a warrior's path. Ultimately what you are renouncing is a life based on your cocoon, motivated only by your habitual craving for security and your instincts of self-centeredness.

28

A LOVE AFFAIR WITH ALONENESS

At this point, before discussing the Fourth Reminder, I would like to offer a few reflections on my own experience of these timeless teachings. I came of age in the late 1960s and early 1970s. I was a young, idealistic college student during the era when the assassinations of both Kennedy brothers and Martin Luther King Jr. happened and when the Vietnam War started. All these events radicalized my outlook about living in America and about life in general—as it did so many of my contemporaries. When I graduated from college, I taught in the public school system of the Ocean Hill–Brownsville ghetto of New York City—partly out of idealism, partly to avoid military service in a war I opposed. After two years of this I was physically exhausted, and my idealism for social change was tempered, if not obliterated altogether.

I reread *Walden.* Thoreau's example inspired me, and I resolved to move to northern rural Vermont and live a simple life there. Many others my own age were also dropping out of the mainstream at this time. We looked at the society around us and told each other that it was corrupt and harmful and we wanted no part of it. This was the closest my generation could come, at that time, to expressing a sense of renunciation as the Buddha taught it.

With the energy and optimism of youth, we fervently believed that we were the virtuous ones and that our communal expressions of virtue could change the world. We left the suburbs, cities, and ghettoes and headed for the woods. We built our own cabins, grew organic gardens, started food co-ops, got high, closed our eyes, and repeated Sanskrit mantras—striving to transcend.

I myself did this for four years, and I can see clearly, in retrospect, that although it was a useful experience, I didn't learn all that much about what it really means not to cause further harm. Even though I had left the noise of the outer world behind, I took my own noise with me. Like a bacillus I carried the inherited, internalized noise of my conditioning in the society in which I was raised.

This cultural noise seemed to have many discordant, recurrent themes—aggression, competitiveness, and especially the constant need for entertainment. Trying to live with my wife and friends in a simple, quiet, rural environment, I dimly heard these themes echoing endlessly in my subconscious gossip. Nor did my idealistic efforts to live a virtuous life protect me from the ordinary pains of marriage, domesticity, and misunderstandings between friends—much of it my own creation. Still, that internal noise was a mere whisper, relatively speaking, because I had not yet entered fully into a commitment to pay really close attention to my inner world.

NAUSEA FROM ALL THIS SPINNING

The Tibetan word for renunciation is *ngejung*. It literally means "really happening" or "completely becoming." The word conveys a sense of total commitment. You are not dabbling or playing at renunciation; you are entering into it, fully and completely. You gradually come down from your habitual state of mental speed, with its endlessly overlapping patterns of fantasies, expectations, hopes, and fears. There develops a sense of nausea, as one might experience while withdrawing from an addiction or when stepping off a ride at an amusement park. It's a kind of spiritual cold turkey initiation. Suddenly you find yourself standing on still ground when you have become so accustomed to spinning in circles. My teacher called it "nausea with samsara" and preferred to use the word *revulsion* over *renunciation* when offering these teachings.

None of this happened during my "back to the land" years in Vermont, when I renounced the world. Instead, those years passed in a kind of righteous, romantic haze. The life I lived there became another cocoon. I had not yet begun to face my life unconditionally. I was still blaming the world and congratulating myself for having outsmarted it. I was still fantasizing that I was living a spiritual life, despite the pain of all the habitual actions and reactions I still carried with me day to day.

No true commitment to a different way of living could actually happen until I met my spiritual teacher, heard his message, experienced his overwhelming genuineness, and began to do intensive meditation practice. At that point, I was fully initiated into the experience of nausea with my own personal samsara.

RECALLING TORMENT AS MOTIVATION ON THE PATH

The Fourth Reminder describes the nausea in this way:

> The homes, friends, wealth, and comfort of samsara
> are the constant torment of the three sufferings,
> Just like a feast before the executioner
> leads you to your death.
> I will cut desire and attachment and attain
> enlightenment through exertion.[38]

During my first meditation retreat, I practiced for thirty days in succession, ten to twelve hours each day. I had no escape from the claustrophobia of my habitual patterns and kleshas. It was like being forced to ride with a very irritating passenger on a long trip in a small car. I was the passenger. I was also the driver. The retreat was the car. There was nothing to do but to continue moving forward, letting all of this material come up, be experienced, and pass away—like a vivid, ever-changing landscape seen from my passing vehicle.

Finishing one thirty-day intensive, I committed shortly afterward to another, then a third. Slowly the claustrophobia, anxiety, restlessness, speed, and sense of personal melodrama began to lift. By the time the third retreat ended, a subtle but profound shift had begun to take place. The temperature of my boredom dropped.

Hot Boredom and Cool Boredom

The "hot boredom" I at first encountered was the boredom of the addict, marked by the feeling that I would go crazy if I did not find a way to fill the emptiness inside, to experience anything other than what I was currently experiencing. After going through all the symptoms of withdrawal, the "cool boredom" that eventually developed had the quality of settling down, into myself, with less evasion. I began to abandon the need to psychologically channel surf. I stopped looking for a different experience than the one I was having.

Traditionally, this is described as beginning to taste your mind as if it were a cool mountain stream. Its constant flow does not offer entertainment, but it does refresh you in a profound way. When you stop struggling to make your experience of the present moment other than it is, the relaxation that begins to dawn in you is such a relief.

This kind of cool boredom is the blessing of genuine renunciation. It has nothing to do with literally abandoning the world and holing up in a cave for years. It is simply the recognition that the games of your ego-fixation are ultimately hopeless. Even if they seem to work for a while, they will leave you empty-handed in the end.

This realization was the fruit of those three months I spent in group retreat practice, and it left an imprint that has stayed with me ever since.

THE LIVING BUDDHA WITHIN ME

After this initiation among a group of fellow practitioners, I began to do solitary retreats. At first they were only a few days long. As the years passed, they got longer. Unlike group retreat practice where other people offer encouragement, a schedule, and rules, in solitary retreat there was no peer pressure of any kind—no one else to push me to stay with the practice. In these solitary months of meditation, I truly tasted the mind of my teacher—the mind of the living Buddha within me. I entered into a love affair with an aloneness that I had never experienced before and have rarely experienced in a sustained way since. I settled down fully with my own mind. I stopped looking for any feedback from the world to tell me who I truly am. There was no one else there to praise or blame me, or for me to praise or blame.

There was just space: the vastness and beauty of the natural world all around me; the quality of the light as it changed continuously throughout the day; the depth and stillness of the night sky with its countless stars; and especially the shifting moods of stillness and movement, memory and expectation, boredom and elation, joy and sadness that passed day after day through my inner world. Everything was vivid, but nothing was permanent. For the first time, I was content with the endless display of the vast, undivided world around me and within me. My whole being relaxed and rejoiced.

As my teacher wrote once of his own experience of retreat, "Good and bad, happy and sad, all thoughts vanish into emptiness like the imprint of a bird in the sky."[39]

I understood the meaning of this personally and unmistakably for the first time. Far beyond the old loneliness that was so desperate for company or confirmation, I fell in love with an aloneness that was deeply content to be alone. I knew then, and know even more poignantly now in retrospect, that it was only the beginning of my journey without goal. But it was a precious discovery, and it changed my life.

ACKNOWLEDGMENTS

Special thanks to Gregg Campbell and Brett Astor for the generosity, and Rebeca Castella and Braddon Hall for the exertion that helped me write this book.

Efforts from talented and dedicated people have made the publication of this book possible. Thank you to Beth Skelley for her elegant design of both the cover and the interior of the book, to copyeditor Gretel Hakanson and proofreader Alix Whitney Davis for their impeccable work, and to Jerry Gentry for the printing.

To Jennifer Holder, who not only accomplished the developmental editing that showed me exactly what I was trying to say all along, but also seamlessly oversaw every aspect of the production of the book from beginning to end—I owe a special debt of gratitude. Thank you, Jennifer!

NOTES

1. Chögyam Trungpa, *Shambhala: The Sacred Path of the Warrior* (Boulder, CO: Shambhala Publications, Inc., 1984).

2. William Wordsworth, "The World is Too Much with Us" (1807) in *The Norton Anthology of Poetry*, 3rd ed., ed. Jahan Ramazani, Richard Ellmann, and Robert O'Clair (New York: W. W. Norton and Company, 1983).

3. Chögyam Trungpa, *Crazy Wisdom, in The Collected Works of Chögyam Trungpa*, ed. Carolyn Gimian, vol. 5 (Boston: Shambhala Publications, Inc., 2004).

4. Pablo Neruda, "Keeping Quiet" in *Extravagaria: A Bilingual Edition*, trans. Alastair Reid (New York: Noonday Press, 2001).

5. Philip Larkin, "Aubade" in *Collected Poems*, ed. Anthony Thwait (New York: Farrar, Straus and Giroux, 2001).

6. Jean-Paul Sartre, *Being and Nothingness* (Paris: Gallimard, 1943).

7. Albert Camus, *The Myth of Sisyphus*, trans. Justin O'Brien (New York: Penguin Books, 1975).

8. Chögyam Trungpa, *Cutting Through Spiritual Materialism*, ed. John Baker and Marvin Casper (Boston: Shambhala Publications, Inc., 1973).

9. T. S. Eliot, "Burnt Norton" in *Four Quartets* (New York: Harcourt Publishing, 1943).

10. Chögyam Trungpa, *Crazy Wisdom*.

11. Chögyam Trungpa, *Shambhala: The Sacred Path of the Warrior.*

12. Blaise Pascal, *Pensees* (New York: Penguin Classics, 2006).

13. Vasubandhu Bodhisattva and Hsuan Hua, *The Shastra on the Door to Understanding The Hundred Dharmas* (San Francisco: Dharma Realm Buddhist Association, 2007).

14. Chögyam Trungpa, *The Sanity We Are Born With* (Boston: Shambhala Publications, Inc., 2005).

15. Chögyam Trungpa, *The Heart of the Buddha* (Boston: Shambhala Publications, Inc., 1991).

16. Chögyam Trungpa, *Shambhala: The Sacred Path of the Warrior.*

17. William Shakespeare, *The Tragedy of Julius Caesar,* 2.2, 1599.

18. Rainer Maria Rilke, *Letters to A Young Poet (#8)* (Leipzig, Germany: Insel Verlag, 1929).

19. W. H. Auden, "September 1, 1939" in *Another Time* (New York: Random House, 1940).

20. Paul Tillich, *Political Expectation* (Macon, GA: Mercer University Press, 1981).

21. Irvin Yalom, *Existential Psychotherapy* (New York: Basic Books, 1980).

22. Chögyam Trungpa, *The Truth of Suffering and the Path of Liberation,* ed. Judith Lief (Boston: Shambhala Publications, Inc., 2009).

23. William Blake, "Eternity" (1800–1808) in *The Norton Anthology of Poetry,* 3rd ed., ed. Jahan Ramazani, Richard Ellmann, and Robert O'Clair (New York: W. W. Norton and Company, 1983).

24. Alan Watts, *The Wisdom of Insecurity* (New York: Vintage Books, 1968).

25. Shunryu Suzuki, *Zen Mind, Beginner's Mind,* ed. Trudy Dixon (New York: John Weatherhill, Inc., 1970).

26. Billy Collins, "Shoveling Snow with Buddha" in *Picnic, Lightning* (Pittsburgh, PA: University of Pittsburgh Press, 1998).

27. William James, *Selected Writings: 1878–1899: Psychology: Briefer Course* (New York: Harper Torchbooks, 1961).

28. Walt Whitman, "Song of Myself" (1855) in *The Oxford Book of American Poetry* (London: Oxford University Press, 2006).

29. Sister Vajira and Francis Story, trans., *Mahaparinibbana Sutta: Last Days of the Buddha* (Kandy, Sri Lanka: Buddhist Publication Society, 1998).

30. Krishna-Dwaipayana Vyasa, *The Mahabarata,* trans. Kisari Mohan Ganguli, 1883–1896.

31. Thich Nhat Hanh, "Long Live Impermanence," Interview with Lisa Schneider, Dharma Gates, dharmagates.org/long_live_impermanence. html, retrieved May 14, 2014.

32. Robert Frost, "Fire and Ice" in *New Hampshire* (New York: Henry Holt, 1923).

33. Jamgon Kongtrul, *The Torch of Certainty,* (Boston: Shambhala Publications, Inc., 2000).

34. Kongtrul, *The Torch of Certainty.*

35. Henry David Thoreau, *Walden, or Life in the Woods* (Boston: Ticknor and Fields, 1854).

36. Henry David Thoreau, "Last Words" in *Oxford Dictionary of American Quotations* (London: Oxford University Press, 2006).

37. Kongtrul, *The Torch of Certainty.*

38. Kongtrul, *The Torch of Certainty.*

39. Chögyam Trungpa, *The Sadhana of the Embodiment of All the Siddhas* (Berkeley, CA: Shambhala Publications, Inc., 1969).

ABOUT THE AUTHOR

Frank W. Berliner is associate professor of contemplative psychology at Naropa University, where he has taught Buddhist and Western Existential Psychology, and the practice of meditation, since 1995. Mr. Berliner pioneered the teaching of meditation online at Naropa and was the buddhadharma columnist for *Elephant* magazine for six years. His popular memoir, *Falling in Love with A Buddha,* offers his experience as "warrior apprentice" to the Tibetan meditation master Chögyam Trungpa Rinpoche.